Death Nesting

The Heart-Centered Practices of a Death Doula

A Sacred Planet Book

ANNE-MARIE KEPPEL

Bear & Company
Rochester, Vermont

Bear & Company
One Park Street
Rochester, Vermont 05767
www.BearandCompanyBooks.com

Text stock is SFI certified

Bear & Company is a division of Inner Traditions International

Sacred Planet Books are curated by Richard Grossinger, Inner Traditions editorial board member and cofounder and former publisher of North Atlantic Books. The Sacred Planet collection, published under the umbrella of the Inner Traditions family of imprints, includes works on the themes of consciousness, cosmology, alternative medicine, dreams, climate, permaculture, alchemy, shamanic studies, oracles, astrology, crystals, hyperobjects, locutions, and subtle bodies.

Cataloging-in-Publication Data for this title is available from the Library of Congress

ISBN 978-1-59143-482-5 (print)
ISBN 978-1-59143-483-2 (ebook)

Printed and bound in the United States by Lake Book Manufacturing, LLC
The text stock is SFI certified. The Sustainable Forestry Initiative® program promotes sustainable forest management.

10 9 8 7 6 5 4 3 2 1

Text design by Priscilla Baker and Kenleigh Manseau and layout by Priscilla Baker
This book was typeset in Garamond Premier Pro with Arquitecta, Gill Sans, Legacy Sans, and Mrs. Eaves used as display typefaces

To send correspondence to the author of this book, mail a first-class letter to the author c/o Inner Traditions • Bear & Company, One Park Street, Rochester, VT 05767, and we will forward the communication, or contact the author directly at **www.AnneMarieKeppel.com**.

Death Nesting

"Anne-Marie uses the image of nest building to introduce ways to build protective circles of care for dying persons and their loved ones. Her writing is tender and loving. She draws on the insights of psychology, spirituality, and ancient wisdom and also includes a discussion of practical care issues stemming from her years of experience. It is refreshing to encounter an author sensitive to the need for literature on end-of-life issues to confront its rather privileged perspective and begin to address the cultural, class, gender, and racial disparities in end-of-life care. *Death Nesting* will be a valuable support for families facing the loss of a loved one."

JUDITH LIEF, BUDDHIST TEACHER, STUDENT AND EDITOR OF CHÖGYAM
TRUNGPA RINPOCHE, AND AUTHOR OF *MAKING FRIENDS WITH DEATH*

"Anne-Marie has gifted us with an informative, holistic, and comprehensive guide to tending to those who are in the dying season of their lives. The practical guidance, mindfulness practices, herbal recommendations, and storytelling offered in *Death Nesting* empower us to support one another to create a dying experience that reflects our unique lived experience."

ADITI SETHI, M.D., HOSPICE AND PALLIATIVE CARE PHYSICIAN,
END-OF-LIFE DOULA, AND EXECUTIVE DIRECTOR AND
FOUNDER OF THE CENTER FOR CONSCIOUS LIVING & DYING

"A resource guide that will transcend your view on death, dying, and how to be in companionship with Death. This beautiful, sensitive guide is filled with knowledge delivered with tenderness and takes the reader through a journey of learning about stages of death, ways caregivers can be supportive during the transition process, caregiver and client meditations, and calming practices. Anne-Marie has gently normalized a subject seldom addressed, so openly. Written for anyone who may be curious about death work, caregivers, and for all of us who will have that familiar, yet unfamiliar, knock on the door from the intimate stranger we call Death."

SONYA-PRAJNA PATRICK, PH.D., DEATH-TENDING DOULA, MAGICK/
CONJURE WORKER, AND BONE READER

"Anne-Marie's way of navigating death and grief is intentional, nourishing, loving, meditative, and healing. With an attitude of humility and reverence for this sacred passage, her words evoke a sensuous experience for the reader, as she brings to life the essence of death doula service. I highly recommend *Death Nesting* to anyone interested in mindfully holding space for their loved one or for themselves through the process of death."

JADE BRUNEL, FOUNDER OF WAO TEA AND AUTHOR OF
TEA, REMEMBERING THE ESSENCE OF LIFE

"*Death Nesting* is a compassionate manual on approaching death consciously—both our own death and the deaths of those we love. Through the pages of this helpful book, death educator and doula Anne-Marie Keppel gives readers the tools needed to turn the end-of-life process into a beautiful and healing experience. Filled with love and spirit this is a book I will be recommending to my clients whether they are facing death or grieving the loss of a loved one."

SALICROW, PSYCHIC MEDIUM AND AUTHOR OF *SPIRIT SPEAKER*

"As explained in *Death Nesting,* dying can be a time of unknowing while also a journey best guided by deep wisdom and trust—both of which are bolstered by Keppel's anecdotes and explanations. This mindfully constructed book of knowledge gently encourages readers to let go of rigid logic and control as well as embrace all that can be anticipated during the end of life, covering an array of topics from the ineffable to the highly practical and so much in between."

FRANCESCA LYNN ARNOLDY, COMMUNITY DOULA AND AUTHOR OF
THE DEATH DOULA'S GUIDE TO LIVING FULLY AND DYING PREPARED

"Keppel's heart-centered, community-based philosophy establishes her as a leader in the emerging holistic deathcare movement. I recommend *Death Nesting* to all aspiring death doulas, medical professionals serving in end-of-life spaces, hospice volunteers, and, most especially, home caregivers. This is a bedside companion for the tender journey as we walk one another home."

JADE ADGATE, DEATH MIDWIFE AND CURATOR AT THE FAREWELL LIBRARY

"Anne-Marie offers loads of wise and practical guidance for helping, holding, and mindful presence through all that this passage brings for the doula, the dying, and for those who must let them go. Whatever your belief about the afterlife, whatever your previous experience with death and dying, this book invites you to the crossroads, where life meets death—a sacred place of deep gravitas, transformation, and remembrance."

FEARN LICKFIELD, DIRECTOR OF THE
GREEN MOUNTAIN DRUID SCHOOL AND DREAMLAND SANCTUARY

"This is the book those who gravitate toward or find themselves thrust into the death space need. Exploring age-old territory with fresh eyes, Anne-Marie Keppel has encapsulated for us the essence of active caring in full practical and loving description."

LEE WEBSTER, FUNERAL REFORM ADVOCATE AND DIRECTOR OF NEW
HAMPSHIRE FUNERAL RESOURCES & EDUCATION

"*Death Nesting* is refreshing, enlightening, and captivating. It dares to talk deeply and thoroughly about a subject that's barely touched in our society, yet it's a reality that we are all going to have to deal with. This book gives the reader a thoughtful and human perspective on confronting death."

RAFAEL OLIVARES, M.D., VOLUNTEER FOR DOCTORS OF THE WORLD

For my three babes,
Phineas Rhodes, Elsa Isidora, and Amaia Luna

And thank you to my (very own) mother Theresa,
who read this every time I asked her.

Contents

Contents

Foreword

Karen Wyatt, M.D.

I sometimes wonder if future historians will look back upon the previous century as the time when human beings in the developed world forgot how to be with death—a time when we lost the bedside wisdom of countless generations of caregivers who had tended their dying loved ones at home. For within a few short years after the turn of the twentieth century, modern society had relegated the dead to funeral homes, the dying to neglected wards in hospital basements, and the grieving to suffer silently in isolation. The ancient wisdom of caring for the dying and the dead at home had all but faded into oblivion, and death had become a hidden enemy to be ignored and avoided at all costs.

But society has rejected death to its own detriment. For life cannot exist without death, and those who refuse to acknowledge death cannot experience life to the fullest. Without an awareness of death people struggle to find meaning in their lives and never learn that every moment of this existence is precious, simply because it is fleeting. This truth has been apparent to me throughout my work as a hospice doctor, visiting families who made the decision to keep their dying loved ones at home. I recognized that those who participate in the mysteries of the dying process are transformed by witnessing the stark beauty of death. I saw how love thrives when death is embraced rather than scorned.

However, even when families today do their best to care for loved ones at home, there is still a lack of knowledge about how to *be* with the dying during all of the unexpected, challenging, and miraculous moments of this process. I learned this for myself when I was called to care for my own mother at the time of her dying. As a hospice doctor with many years of experience I assumed I knew everything necessary to support my mother in her last days. Yet over and over again I sat at her bedside feeling helpless to assist her on this journey. I knew all about medications I could prescribe but nothing about the hands-on nurturing and supportive care that might have made all the difference. In the middle of a sleepless night I recognized just how much I didn't know and that there was nowhere I could turn at that moment to learn what I needed. Undoubtedly many other caregivers find themselves in similar situations as they confront the challenges of being with a dying loved one.

The book you are currently reading holds the answers I was seeking during those days and nights I spent with my mother. Anne-Marie Keppel has gathered the "lost" wisdom of the old ways of being with the dying and combined it with the best practices of modern home care to craft a guide for all who wish to attend death at the bedside. This book emphasizes that the experience of death is transformational for both the patient and the caregiver, who together weave a delicate dance as the last moments of life unfold. There are practices to create a sacred space for the patient and assist with the physical, emotional, and spiritual aspects of the dying process, including herbal therapies contributed by Sandra Lory. For the caregiver this book contains mindfulness meditations, numerous practical tips for self-care, and advice for handling the unexpected and sometimes distressing situations that might arise during the dying process.

Whether you are a practicing death doula or a layperson facing the task of caring for a loved one, *Death Nesting* is the resource needed to rediscover the knowledge that was once abandoned by modern society. When we acquaint ourselves with the naturalness of death and invite it back into our awareness, we can restore the balance and meaning of all of life, taking nothing for granted and treating all beings with care. As we struggle with war, climate devastation, a global pandemic, and social injustice on this planet, we can surely all benefit from this wisdom that honors the sacredness of both life and death and guides us toward greater harmony in this natural cycle of existence.

As for my caregiving experience with my mother, I managed to find within me my own intuitive guidance on the very last night of her life. I awoke from a light sleep with the realization that she hadn't called out to me or rung the little bell on her nightstand for a few hours. When I went to check on her I found that her breathing had already become irregular and I knew she wouldn't be with me much longer. I started to cry because I wasn't ready for our journey together in this mysterious portal of death to come to an end. I wanted to experience more of the incredible love that we had just begun to share. Yet the timing wasn't up to me. Not knowing what else to do in that moment, I crawled into her bed and cradled her bent body into mine, creating a safe nest for her to relax into. She briefly opened her eyes, smiled, and patted my arm that encircled her. As she had so often held me when I needed comfort, I was finally able to hold her and shower her with my love while she continued her own inner work of leaving behind her physical form. This memory is what comes to me when I think of "death nesting"—this space of ultimate safety and sacredness where life can dissolve into pure love.

As you set out to read this book, remember to start wherever you are. If death is a stranger to you, begin by gradually absorbing the information in these pages. Allow this wisdom to enter your consciousness and then be willing to sit with your own discomfort in dealing with the unknown and frightening aspects of death. You may find that something ancient awakens deep within you—a part of you that has always been present and recognizes the rightful place of death within this life. If you are caring for a dying loved one, you may find, as I did, that you are capable instinctively of doing what is necessary in the moment. Let this book empower you to be present for those who need you as they make their final journey. Let it help you prepare for your own last great transformation by living a death-aware life for all the rest of your days.

KAREN WYATT, M.D., is the bestselling author of the book *7 Lessons for Living from the Dying*, which contains stories of patients she cared for as a hospice doctor and the spiritual lessons she learned from them at the end of their lives. Dr. Wyatt also hosts the podcast *End-of-Life University*, which features conversations with experts who work in all aspects of end-of-life care. She is widely regarded as a thought-leader in the effort to transform the way we care for our dying in the United States.

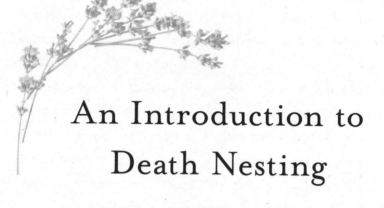

An Introduction to Death Nesting

This is a good time to notice your breathing.
In and out, in and out . . .

*D*eath nesting is about preparing the nest for one who is dying, just as we might prepare a nest for one who is about to give birth. Some individuals begin "nesting" before menstruation or during pregnancy in preparation for birth. Once the environment feels safe, orderly, and ready, a spaciousness opens for the internal work to begin and the release to happen.

When you consider the construction of a nest, it is quite similar to the care that should be taken to make way for death. The coarse, outer pieces of straw and mud form the hard protective shell, while the soft, fine materials inside comfort the chicks. This is similar to the womb of mammals, and then bassinets that we put our babies in. Among humans and in nature, we prepare sacred spaces for sacred acts. Just as we prepare safe and comfortable birthing spaces, we should create safe and comfortable deathing spaces.

Besides the physical space that we should prepare for an imminent death, we each prepare our nests for death in our everyday lives. How we live, where we live, who we interact with, how we care for ourselves and others, whether or not we have intimate partners, children or no children—these and economic, cultural, racial, and societal challenges all will play a role in our death. Whether our deaths are sudden, unexpected, or prolonged, the story of how they impact our world and others' will be determined by how we lived. The ways in which our communities rally to support us (or turn away) through our dying, and how they support each other (or do not support each other) after we are no longer living, will be influenced by how we lived our lives.

The time I take now to contemplate and make arrangements for my death (while I am not in the emotional throes of actively dying) will undoubtedly help my future self—or at least those who love me. For instance, I have regularly written love letters to my children since they were born. I have told them how proud I am of them and requested that they please be gentle and loving with themselves and others, and to take healthy risks. On a daily basis I try to say "thank you" as often as I can, and "I'm sorry" when I have hurt someone or something. Even if I'm still mad at the individual, I will say, "I am still really angry right now, but I care for you very much." If my death is sudden, I have covered all my bases so that I can release without fear or attachment. If I have a slower death, I will have fewer regrets, apologies, and concerns—I'll be able to turn inward more easily in order to comfort myself for my grand release.

Death nesting is how you live your life *now*, for it is a greater challenge to have a "good death" if you have not lived a "good life." We tend to take refuge in money, relationships, health, things that offer certainty or security—but none of those are comforts the dying can rely upon. Engaging in death nesting throughout your life by doing things such as studying death and dying and caring for or volunteering to work with the dying will help prepare your mind and inform you about practicalities and the spiritual aspects for your own dying time. A good life could simply be actively recognizing and taking pleasure in things like watching animals move in their habitat, listening to the sounds of nature, easily getting yourself a glass of water, or noticing that your heart beats regularly, as it should. Sometimes those kinds of simple profundities might only be fully appreciated after working with the dying.

I'm concerned that many people newly interested in death and dying think that naming powers of attorney and listing funeral and disposition preferences is making progress in acknowledging their mortality. Although those *can* be helpful things to do, I've seen loved ones in turmoil after a death when an elaborate request has been made that is difficult or impossible to fulfill. Yes, get your affairs in order and list your preferences for medical and postmortem care, but always end with something along the lines of, "Thank you for making an effort, even if these requests cannot be fulfilled."

Rather than planning every last detail of your funeral (though that can be fun), make the effort to be sure people will *attend* your funeral by valuing and embodying kindness, strength in vulnerability, and generosity toward yourself and others. Talk about death and dying so that when you die, your friends, family, community, and coworkers will know that it is totally acceptable to talk about their feelings with each other after you're gone. By living your life while embracing your death, you are giving others permission to do the same.

As you read through these pages you will encounter

reminders of your own mortality. In this way, you are preparing a nest of awareness and appreciation for your own precious life while also engaging empathetically so that you can clearly and humbly work with one who is dying.

Let's begin with a mindfulness practice in gentleness. You will need this as you read through the book and when you are working with one who is dying. I recommend making this mindfulness practice a part of your regular routine in life; part of your individual death nesting. You may find yourself becoming quite sad while you do this exercise; that is okay—love yourself through your sadness.

You can be taught to be kind to others, but you can only be truly, genuinely, deeply gentle with others when you are truly, genuinely, deeply gentle with yourself. This does not mean you are lazy in your gentleness and become blasé or passive in a nonstop state of gentle kindness and acceptance. Rather, you are awake, attentive, and intentionally generous in your gentleness. Eventually, after practicing this kindness with yourself and others, it will become second nature. You will find yourself experiencing less compassion fatigue if you practice this core mindfulness practice regularly.

❧❀❧

MINDFULNESS PRACTICE
Nesting Meditation

Sit in a comfortable position, preferably with a straight spine. You want to remain upright so you do not fall asleep, but you also should be comfortable. Find a balance, both soft and alert.

Imagine your sit bones rooted in the earth. A small invisible thread pulls from the top of your head and leads straight up through the atmosphere into the unknown.

Begin by imagining yourself as a newly born infant. All earthly sensations are brand new: lights are overwhelming, sounds are tremendous, smells are foreign, tastes are shocking. Even your own limbs flailing about are startling. From this very first moment, each of us begins a very different path. What was your path? Were you welcomed into your mother's arms? Did another care for you? How did your years unfold?

As you follow the path of your story, hold great loving-kindness and compassion for yourself. In many ways, even as an adult, you are a child on the earth. Using your imagination, hold yourself, the newborn, in your cupped palm. Place your other cupped palm over the top so you are holding the image of your infant self safely in a loving nest, in your wise and gentle hands.

Hold yourself in this same loving nest through childhood, adolescence, and adulthood. Hold yourself in soft kindness through all your life's challenges, understanding that your life is a story. Your entire life is a story for which you can hold great compassionate love—even through your mistakes, even through unkindnesses that you have inflicted. Know that you are basically good. You have challenges just like everyone else on the earth. You have sadnesses, fears, heartbreaks, and traumas (seen and unseen) just like everyone else.

Hold yourself gently, kindly; offer this same generosity to those around you. Eventually, you may be able to do this practice for your community, your country, and the planet.

❦

About This Book

*T*his book is written primarily with a one-on-one caregiver/care-receiver model in mind, but ideally a whole village would take part. The phrases "your loved one" and "the one dying" are used interchangeably to reduce redundancy.

We will begin with advance directives, ceremony, and explanations of the outer, inner, and secret nests along with how to prepare the environment for the one dying. The next chapters lead you through the senses during the dying process and what the physical body does during dying. Acknowledged after that are the rather uncomfortable circumstances that can arise with difficult family dynamics and tough decision-making. Toward the end of the book, there is a chapter about how to talk to children about death and dying, and then we finish with what happens after the last breath and some thoughts on moving with grief. A closing meditation is also provided, inspired by the Buddhist dissolution practice.

The care described in this book incorporates both ancient and modern death doula techniques and can be implemented by any person who intends to care for another. You do not need a specific title to "doula" someone while they are dying—simply a willingness to physically, emotionally, mentally (and perhaps spiritually) accompany an individual through this process. There are occasional references to being a death doula, if you consider yourself such. An appendix at the back of the book provides more information about the work of a death doula, including a look at the divide between what I call the *ancient death doula* and the *modern death doula*. In brief, an ancient death doula is one who has learned through hands-on experience and family or community modeling. A modern death doula is one who has taken a death doula course and may be knowledgeable but may not have any care experience.

- **The ancient death doula** has had no formal death doula training but has grassroots life experience of intimately caring for people through the dying process. They may weave more spiritual, healing, or ancient practices into their deathcare regime. (I do not consider one who is just *interested* in this to be an ancient death doula, though a cellular remembering is undoubtedly a start.)
- **The modern death doula** has completed one or more death doula certificate trainings and may be more focused professionally and better acquainted with the modern demands of dying and death.

. . . .

Note: Be advised that there is a big difference between being a volunteer caregiver or death doula and being a paid caregiver or death doula (whether or not the one dying is a family member). At times, when a fee is charged there are legal issues that can arise. This book is simply a guide for caring for the dying—with tales from my own experiences. By no means is it intended to be used as any kind of medical, legal, therapeutic, or funeral advice. Every state, province, and country has its own laws and you must do your due diligence to research and abide by these regulations.

. . . .

Since much of my knowledge is experience-based, I often add anecdotes to paint a fuller picture or to support the care suggestions. Everything in this book is based on my own experiences and work.

I am writing from the perspective of a white woman of Irish Celtic and Finnish Sámi (Indigenous European) ancestry and realize that my perspective is biased in this reality. There are, of course, many possible cultural perspectives surrounding this work. I have chosen to focus on what I believe is universal.

The bulk of this book is about how to relate to the body directly, beyond the wealth of implicit cultural assumptions that accompany death and dying around the world. One who cares for someone dying in New Guinea, Peru, or Siberia will have certain beliefs about this process, but all humans will have an erratic heartbeat or struggle with breathing during their last moments on Earth.

I am aware that the kind of dying considered in this book is quite privileged. There are so many on our planet who will never have this kind of thoughtful, loving care. There are many who die in war-torn lands, as environmental or political refugees, by the hand of racists, without pain medications available, addicted, isolated or unhoused, without a hand to hold or anyone to notice they are gone. This may not be my daily reality or yours, but we should not be immune to this devastation. The dying wish of a woman I cared for was that when we washed and dressed her dead body, we should hold in our hearts the refugees who will never receive that kind of care. She did not name it as such, but in my Buddhist tradition we call this "dedicating the merit." While engaging in an activity that could be considered fortunate, we expand our love, kindness, and generosity to all beings who need to be liberated from suffering. We cannot physically care for every being on the planet, but we can bring others into our awareness while making an effort to better our world where and when we can.

Please consider the whole human, just as they are, as you implement care. There are many holistic, nurturing ideas in this book, but not every individual will be comfortable with these approaches. Take into consideration the culture, ethnicity, race, class, sex, and gender identity of the individual you are caring for, without making judgments or assumptions. This is particularly important if you do not know the one you are caring for very well. Make an effort to learn how they lived. Respect their needs, their story, the choices they made in life, and be mindful of pushing your own ideals on them through the dying process or after death.

For example, someone who is accustomed to modest surroundings may not feel comfortable moving to a lavish setting. It may seem like a wonderful way to "treat" someone at the end of their days, but it might make them feel uncomfortable. Sometimes at-home deathcare entails a move into the home of another—elderly parents moving in with their children, or terminally ill adults moving in with their parents. These moves are hard on everyone.

This book focuses on intimate care, ideas for showing kindness, little vignettes, and encouragement for you (the caregiver or doula). It offers small glimpses into the world of nonmedical dying and death—including practices such as Reiki, spirit guidance, herbalism, ceremony, magic, and ways of recognizing the elements and flow of nature in the dying process. It also covers practical techniques for physical care.

As you read, consider the entire ecosystem of the dying process, both the living beings and nonliving supports in and around the dying environment—and how they interact with each other. Look at different situations from different angles, use different lenses to implement different kinds of care if something is not flowing easily. The herbal supports, nursing tips, and mindfulness practices are intended to be helpful and not cause additional stress. If something is not a good fit for your situation or is too complex, simply eliminate it from your toolkit or routine and move on. The goal is to produce comforting results.

You will do the best you can and things will unfold as they will. If we were able to die once as a trial run and then do it again after some reflection, we would become experts. How poignant that there is no dress rehearsal, only a final performance and exit.

HERBAL SUPPORT IN THIS BOOK

Throughout this book, my friend Sandra Lory—a gifted herbalist, R.N., and caregiver—has added information about herbal support for both the one who is dying and the caregiver. Sandra was raised in Vermont but was born in Chennai, India, and inherited her gift with herbs from her maternal grandmother, who was a village herbalist in Goa. Sandra has been the caregiver for her own aging and ailing parents and has worked on many projects in traditional and ancestral medicine, disaster relief through herbalism, and food as medicine initiatives in India, Haiti, Palestine, Venezuela, Mexico, Puerto Rico, and the United States.

The world of herbal healing and care is immense. You'll notice that although herbs play a healing role in these pages, they are used for soothing, supporting, and loving without trying to repair the physical body or mimic allopathic medicines. A great deal of healing can transpire through the dying process; as caregivers, we can offer a healing space while nourishing the spirit of the one dying as they transition out of life. Herbal aids are wonderful midwives that assist us with transitions, and they can inspire creativity and ways of working with nature while dying. Note that not all herbs are readily available, and some essential oils can be expensive. Whenever possible, it is best to use what is growing locally (in a pesticide-free area). Check to see if the one who is dying has any allergies before implementing herbal care, and always consult with a medical doctor.

MINDFULNESS PRACTICES

In some chapters, I list a mindfulness practice that can be done. *Mindfulness* is another word for meditation that leans more toward an active state. For example, I suggest a mindfulness practice for handwashing. This means that you hold your focus on washing your hands in that moment instead of washing your hands while thinking of all of the other things you need to do. These practices are suggested in order to connect you with what you are doing in that moment and to support your general well-being (as caring for the dying can be quite difficult at times).

You may find that doing one mindfulness practice a day is helpful. You may find that once per week is sufficient. In a rough patch, you may wish to engage in a practice several times throughout the day. However, remember to be gentle with yourself in terms of how often you believe you should be doing these practices. If you find that you really enjoy mindfulness or meditation, you may wish to do an extended retreat one day.

You certainly do not need to do the mindfulness practices, but maybe you'll find one that feels like a good fit for you. If you choose only one, I suggest the Nesting Meditation on page 4.

ALTERNATIVE LOCATION REFERENCES

We do not all end up dying in the place where we plan. While this book focuses on bedridden care at home, there are suggestions for incorporating holistic care into other environments that you may find yourself in.

CHALLENGES IN CARING FOR YOUR OWN DYING

The thought of caring for a dying loved one in their home or your own can be daunting. In some instances, it may not be possible. While dying at home was the only real option for families before the 1920s' hospital boom in the United States, when the modern miracles of medicine (namely, antibiotics) became widely available families began entrusting their dying loved ones to hospitalized care. Steadily increasing over the decades, hospitals became the most common place of death for Americans until a decrease in the past fifteen years, when more Americans have been dying at home. A 2020 report from the CDC stated that about 31 percent of people now die at home.* Although a large majority of Americans say that home is their preferred place to die, being a part of that 31 percent does not necessarily correlate to getting better care—this greatly depends on the circumstances. However, with increasing education and awareness in our culture of death, dying, and end-of-life care, perhaps there will be more people who are willing and able to care for dying family, friends, and community members.

Some pockets in the United States that are overwhelmingly poor and/or primarily Black or of another racially or ethnically marginalized group face great challenges with end-of-life care. In particular, writer and historian Cynthia Greenlee, Ph.D., writes, "Communities of color lag in accessing end-of-life care—whether because of cultural beliefs, experience and well-founded fear of racism in medical settings, lack of insurance or financial resources, or misconceptions about what's available."† An excellent book to read more on this topic is *Medical*

---

*"QuickStats: Percentage of Deaths, by Place of Death—National Vital Statistics System, United States, 2000–2018." *Morbidity and Mortality Weekly Report* 69, no. 19 (2020): 611.
†Greenlee, Cynthia. "How Death Doulas Ease the Final Transition." *Yes!* (Fall 2019: The Death Issue).

Apartheid by Harriet A. Washington. (See the resources list at the end of this book for additional recommendations.)

I have hopes that our society will begin to *treasure* end-of-life care and make social, political, financial, and educational adjustments, including racial and cultural sensitivity training, to make it a greater possibility for more individuals.

STAGES AND LEVEL OF CARE

There are various considerations to bear in mind, depending on the stage of dying and the mobility level of the individual. To care for a loved one who is still semi-mobile and uses the toilet may require support from more than one caregiver, as trips to the bathroom or from bed to a favorite chair can be physically taxing. This book focuses on bedridden care, with few or no transfers to the bathroom or elsewhere. Although we mainly focus on home deathcare without much support from professional staff, accepting assistance from hospice can sometimes be what makes or breaks the ability to care for your loved one at home.

Another consideration is the mental state of your loved one. If they are combative or wandering at night, you will likely need support so that you, the caregiver, are able to get adequate sleep and avoid excessive worry and physical exhaustion. General fears, agitations, and suggestions for care are discussed in chapter 5.

If the individual you are caring for has created a death plan, comprehensive advance directive, or ethical will, use that as a guide as you prepare the nest. Their plan will help you create an environment, ambience, and model of care that is most soothing for them.

If your loved one is able to talk, you can ask them to guide these preparations. If they are unable to communicate or only communicate a little, look for signs of comfort or discomfort and make adjustments as needed. Depending on which stage of dying they are in, they may take little or no notice of the room or your efforts. Do not despair. Their internal dying process is not about you. They are simply turning their energy inward as they comfort themselves internally.

Make note of your efforts. The work you are doing—though it may feel daunting, confusing, or tiresome—is the work that makes life precious. Caring for the dying has all the ingredients needed to create movement toward expanding your appreciation for life, but you need the right amount of each effort. Too much worry and you will become overly stressed. Not enough sleep and you may find yourself out of balance mentally and emotionally. Keep a journal of what you are doing so that if things become confusing or overly stressful for you, a helpful friend could review your efforts, find where the imbalance might be, and help implement a remedy for your own ailment as caregiver. There are suggestions for self-care and moving with grief in chapter 8.

IF YOU ARE NOT CURRENTLY CARING FOR SOMEONE DYING

If you are not currently caring for someone but are simply curious or looking for information, consider drafting your advance directive while you read this book. There are straightforward advance directives that can be downloaded for free online or obtained at your doctor's office. The following chapter provides additional information, and throughout this book you will find other comprehensive approaches to care that can be added to the basic form. Be sure to include miscellaneous but important information such as passwords for online banking and social media accounts. Consider storing these in a safety deposit box or other secure location.

When making end-of-life plans, it's a good idea to follow through with details of your final disposition. Looking into your options could be a family activity (if you can get everyone on board), or even an entertaining date night! You might have fun discovering the variety of possibilities, such as green burial, home burial, human composting, alkaline hydrolysis, and open air cremation (pyre). Which options are legal and offered in your area? Which are not yet legal but on the horizon?

A woman in my town knows that she wants to be cremated. Her family laughed when she told them she wants her ashes to be divvied up into her mother's antique salt and pepper shakers. Her deceased mother's vintage collection is precious to her and she wants to ensure her loved ones each get a portion of her cremains. What better way to do this than to give everyone a sweet little shaker of grandma? "Just sprinkle me here and there, wherever you'd like," she says.

If you have not participated in hospice volunteer training, I highly recommend it. The training itself is helpful, and volunteering can be really rewarding—even life-changing. It's helpful to become familiar with dying while under a professional umbrella like hospice, where you feel supported in your efforts. This is a great way to gain experience caring for the dying and to learn how different each household is. There is nothing like walking into a home that feels comfortable to the person there but smells, sounds, and feels completely foreign to you—though it might just be your neighbor—and the one job you have is to be kind, open, helpful, and nonjudgmental.

One of the sweetest dying wishes I assisted with as a hospice volunteer was bringing a basket of kittens to a woman who was dying. Becoming familiar with death in gentle ways like this can help you make paths through the field so that when it is your time to care for someone you love, you can at least see the tracks from your previous experiences.

May this book offer you the encouragement to care for your own dying, engage you in comforting thoughts about your own death, and help you prepare the nest for both. May our world be better for your loving efforts.

One

Beyond Advance Directives

Love in its fullest form is a series of deaths and rebirths.
CLARISSA PINKOLA ESTÉS

An advance directive or living will is a document completed by you regarding the kind of medical care you would like to receive along with emergency contacts, end-of-life preferences, and sometimes your values and disposition choice. This is helpful information for your next of kin and doctor, and maybe your friends and family, to have in the instance that you are no longer able to communicate for yourself. As we are often told, it can also be the best way not to be a burden on your loved ones, so that they do not have to guess at what your end-of-life preferences might be. Working on your own advance directive in conjunction with reading this book could be very helpful. Note that every state and province has its own regulations regarding the use of advance directives and living wills—inquire with your doctor.

. . . .

Terminology Explained

The terms *advance directive* and *living will* are sometimes used interchangeably. There are some differences, however, even though both documents relate to medical care.

Living Will

A living will is a document that you create for yourself in regard to the kind of end-of-life care you would prefer. This will include things such as medical treatments—for how long and in what ways you wish to have your life extended, if possible.

Advance Directive

An advance directive is a bit more general and covers the times when you may not be able to advocate for yourself. It is not just for those who have a terminal diagnosis or are nearing end of life. An advance directive can be completed by young and healthy individuals who wish to name their primary contact person in case of an emergency such as a stroke or car accident.

Medical Orders

A do-not-resuscitate order, or DNR, means that medical professionals are not to revive you if you die. This is not a part of the living will document. It is separate and is a medical order that only a doctor can approve. Doctors also create orders such as do not intubate (DNI), which bars medical professionals from extending your life via intubation. More comprehensive orders are available for those who have been diagnosed with a serious illness. These go by different names, including portable order for life-sustaining treatment (POLST), medical order for life-sustaining treatment (MOLST), and transportable physician orders for patient preferences (TPOPP). Set up an appointment with your doctor to find out more.

Medical Power of Attorney

A medical power of attorney (MPOA), sometimes called a medical agent or proxy or healthcare POA, is designated when creating an advance directive or living will. This should be someone you trust to make the right decisions for you. If the person you wish to designate would not be considered the closest next of kin (such as spouse, parent, or adult child), it is important that you clearly document this proclamation and alert the necessary parties so there is no confusion amid an emergency. This can be very sensitive work! Talk with your doctor, friends, and family and consider who would be the best person to act as your MPOA. The best medical power of attorney for you is not necessarily your next of kin. An MPOA may have some of the following attributes:

- Can remain somewhat clearheaded when receiving sensitive news
- Is in the same time zone as you or will pick up the phone at any hour
- Answers the phone—has a cell phone and/or is always by a phone

- Speaks the same language as you or is able to translate if need be
- Has reliable transportation or a means of travelling easily
- Able to communicate effectively and advocate for your wishes if need be

Ethical Will

An ethical will, sometimes referred to as legacy work or a legacy letter, is a beautiful way to share with your loved ones the things that you love or the things that make you *you* in your life. This is a document or letter that holds your thoughts, your wishes, your aspirations. It can contain favorite recipes, funny jokes or stories, your favorite kind of weather, and favorite scents. It can share your regrets, the losses you have experienced, times of great hardship, and how you coped. This document can be the same or separate from your disposition (or final resting place) and funeral preferences. Ethical wills can be treasures that are passed on for generations and keep your name alive long after you have departed earth.

. . . .

The factors and circumstances surrounding preparation for each death are as varied and unique as each life. For individuals who have claimed their gender identity over their assigned sex at birth, clear advance directives are important in expressing how they would like their body cared for and which pronouns to use throughout the dying process—all the way to the wording on their headstone. Support from respectful caregivers and funeral directors is also important.

Be aware that advance directives are not always followed in emergency situations and sometimes what you have listed as a preference may not be possible, depending on the scenario. The best way to be sure your advance directive is followed is to regularly update it to reflect your current health condition. Be sure to date it, sign it, and replace old copies with the updated version so that there is no confusion. Commonly, your primary physician should have a copy, along with your medical agent(s), and of course you should keep one yourself. Make a list of who you have given a copy to so that everyone receives the most recent updates.

While caring for your loved one you may have come across their advance directive, or you might inquire if they have one. This is a very good place to start when beginning to determine what kind of care your loved one would like to receive and how to build their nest to their liking. Be sure to note the date the directive was written and check in with your loved one about the details, if possible, as preferences may have changed over time or circumstance.

TAKE NOTES

As you care for the dying you will begin to categorize things you like and don't like about the given situation. The one you are caring for may be receiving more meds than you yourself would like during your dying process. Or you may notice that the level of activity in the room is to a degree that you personally find disruptive. While the time caring for the dying is about *their* feelings, preferences, and lifestyle, it can be helpful when on your own time to make notes about your personal preferences. These can be incorporated in an ethical or living will, separate from the more medical formalities of a state-issued advance directive.

Even if you are not currently caring for someone who is dying, working on an advance directive can feel good to do with friends and family—and it helps everyone understand that their dying time will come one day as well. This can be an intimate group activity, an opportunity to share references and stories. You may feel as though caring for the dying—or even thinking about dying—is very serious business, but some of my best laughs have been with the dying or with their caregivers as we share stories and commiserate during such a tense time. I highly encourage some healthy belly laughing if at all possible. Psychic tears of joy, not just sorrow, can feel good to release as well.

If you work on your advance directive by yourself, go gently. It's tough work to be asked what your social security number is on one page and whether or not you'd like a feeding tube on the next page. I recommend doing the Nesting Meditation (page 4) while you engage in this kind of sensitive work. If you have specific questions about your advance directive, you can make an appointment with a doctor or lawyer to ask those questions. Note that advance directives vary greatly in each state and province; they are not all the same. Find the one(s) appropriate for your region. A living will or advance directive can also be a part of your estate planning (contact a financial professional for that work) and the paperwork can be filed altogether so that your loved ones have everything in one place.

During the outbreak of COVID-19 at the beginning of 2020, many of those who had completed their advance directives suddenly panicked. Many people had stated in the document that they did not wish to have a breathing or feeding tube. But when they filled out those forms, they were not anticipating a pandemic. The chaos that ensued in hospitals and health centers around the world left people feeling powerless, and very scared. Loved ones who went into the hospital might never be seen again—ever. There were no visitors allowed at all, people could not get through to contact patients once they were in the hospital, and even after they died (if they died) there would be little to no chance of ever seeing their body. Those in the hospital and their loved ones barred from the hospital were terrified that final moments would be spent alone, in pain, confused, perhaps even in a hallway.

Keep in mind that in places of privilege this lack of access is largely unheard of, so during the pandemic it was traumatizing on a large scale. Yet dying alone is not uncommon. People die alone in their houses from heart attacks and in car accidents on the side of the road. People die under bridges, in alleyways, in war zones, and in storms—alone. You may think, yes, but I am not one of those people. But, in truth, we do not get to choose our manner of death. Gently holding an understanding of death and dying around the world can help us to be grateful for the options of care and comfort that we have available to us.

MORE THAN JUST PAPERWORK

While reading this or while working on an advance directive you could suddenly be afraid that your death might be closer than you thought it was going to be, or you may imagine what it would be like to die alone. These are natural feelings that everyone has when they sit down to complete this paperwork. And if you are currently caring for a dying loved one, it has most certainly brought all of this to the surface.

But, take comfort. I will share with you a secret: all of the plans and written instructions are not the most powerful part of advance directive work. Something magical is possible when you do the work to plan for your dying—but it is invisible. If you have been around someone who is dying, you understand that there's a lot more going on than just the mundane. It's more than paperwork and visitor preferences. It's more than the lighting, the sounds, the smells, and your favorite quilt. Dying is curious, unknown, mystical, and we have little idea what is going on inside the mind of the one dying. Let's look beyond the instructions of the advance directive and examine what is not written there.

⚜

MINDFULNESS PRACTICE
Guided Contemplation

Here is an exercise to try on your own. After you become comfortable with this practice, if you are working with someone who is dying you can lead them through it too by asking questions about their "room." Remember, though, what might feel simple to you in your healthy state or as the caregiver might feel invasive or presumptuous to the one dying. If you think that the exercise would be of value, you could always ask, Would it feel good to do a guided contemplation for comfort with me?

Imagine a room in your home that is locked, and you have never gone in it. You carry the key in your pocket, but you never have the time to open that door. Or maybe you have plenty of time to open it, but you're not sure what you're going to find in there, so you think it's best to just keep it locked. Maybe some days you hear a thump in that room, and it makes your heart race. You think, maybe I should open the door. *You pause, waiting for another thump, but when it doesn't happen you continue on with your life and put off the investigation for another day. This can go on for years, even for an entire lifetime.*

One day you find yourself on the other side of that door, completely confused. You're not sure how you got there, and you think, how did this happen? This is not how I planned to open this door!

Here's an alternative: This evening, when you feel tender but brave, unlock that door. If your fears and imagination try to stop you, hold steady, turn the key in the lock and press on. When you enter, you may be surprised because it is not dark and dusty and scary. There are no ghosts, no cobwebs. Nothing jumps out at you. Instead, it is simply an ordinary room. It's neither new nor old, hot nor cold, light nor dark. In fact, it feels like nothing more than possibility.

Looking around the room, you decide that there should be a bed, and suddenly a bed appears. You sit on the bed, and it creaks in a familiar way. You settle down, realizing that you are in your own blankets, and you say, Ah, this is my bed. *As you lie there, you think that it would be nice to have a window open so you can hear the birds. And before you can blink, a window opens. There is a little warm breeze, a stream of light, and the room fills with gentle birdsong. You smile. You think there should be a little chair, over there, for someone to sit next to you and read aloud. And it is so. You get comfortable and your mind drifts.*

You glance at the walls of this room—your room in this personal, liminal realm—and you think that there should be some photos there. You think of all of your loved ones on earth. Then you think of all of your loved ones who have died before you. You think there should be photos of both on the walls, because, after all, in this space—as in dying—you are neither fully alive nor fully dead. You smile at your own cleverness and instantly the walls fill with photos of everyone you have ever loved.

But up pops one that makes you hesitate. Ugh. Do you really want that person's photo on the wall? You got in such a terrible fight last week. But you're surprised, because in this room you notice that your feelings are different. You're not so angry. You're not in such a hurry here. In fact, you can't really remember what your argument was about. You conclude that you would like to have this photo on the wall. You decide that you'd like to apologize to this person now. You decide that you actually want to tell this person that you love them.

Now you have done several things. You've planned your ideal dying, not just the medical details—such as whether or not you'd like a feeding tube, hydration, or antibiotics—but, more importantly, you have discovered things about your living that will make a difference on your deathbed. You also found a place of comfort, within your own mind, regarding your dying.

You felt it, you smelled it, you heard it, and because you imagined it once, you can certainly imagine it again. No matter where you are or who you are with (or not with), you have the power to rebuild that comfort in your own mind, regardless of your external circumstances, and a peaceful death is possible. Leave the other details up to the living. They have their own work to do, and that's okay. Your dying can be absolutely anything you imagine if you are mindful of your preferences and desires while you're living. And that is what makes advance directive work so important—especially if you're able to look and feel beyond the questions on the paper.

Two

Preparing the Nest

The more you nurture a feeling of loving kindness, the happier and calmer you will be.

DALAI LAMA

Ideally, a community of caregivers would come together to protect the nesting area for the one dying. Since there are many personalities that come together to offer this care, it can be helpful to organize based on the individual gifts of each member. Some people are best at scheduling and making phone calls, some prefer housekeeping or ceremonial work. In this chapter, we'll look at the many ways to create a nurturing environment for the one dying.

ESTABLISHING THE PROTECTIVE SHELL

In places of ceremony, some sort of protection is often intentionally established to keep the hectic outside world from entering the sacred inner space. In the wild, creatures sound an alarm when a potential predator comes close to a nesting site. Elephants will often stand guard around one who is sick or close to death. Dying is a sacred ceremonial act, and if possible, we should try to set up a protective barrier and create a safe container for it.

Listed below are practical suggestions that may be appropriate for caregivers to implement. Some of these can be the tasks of a modern death doula.

- Set up an autoresponse in your email account explaining that you have limited or no availability at this time. You can do the same with your voicemail or answering machine.
- If the one dying has a social media presence, write down the passwords and store them in a safe place. You may want to post something about the condition of your loved one in advance of their death. (Even if you do not post beforehand, knowing this password and assigning someone to the accounts as backup can be helpful.) A regular community gathering place, such as a church, club, or bar, can be a more intimate place to post specific requests for prayers, Reiki, or love.
- Ask a friend who is not directly caring for the dying person to communicate with the outside world. In some instances, you might have one point person who then communicates with two others—one for each side of the extended family. Relaying information in this way protects you from receiving dozens of inquiries.
- Ask a reliable friend to retrieve and sort through your mail. If you trust them, request that they open the mail and organize it according to priority.
- Ask someone to coordinate a meal train. Cooking might be pleasurable, but there will be times when grocery shopping

and preparing food might be difficult. Request that meals be portioned out for easy heating and freezing.

- A sign on the front door can help neighbors understand what's going on. Without providing copious amounts of information (unless that is appropriate), you can list good times for visiting and request that space be given at all other hours.

- Make a list of the dying person's regular activities and responsibilities. If they have children who go to school and after-school programs, for example, perhaps a transportation chart would be helpful. Are there chores on the farm or pets that need to be tended to? Again, some kind of chart can be helpful to explain that the dog has to go for a walk every day or else will bark all evening.

- A caregiver stipend could be created to ease the financial burdens of those doing the active, sometimes nonstop care. The primary caregiver may not be able to work at all during the active dying process, which can create additional stress not only for them but for the one dying. Pooling money to be given can be a lovely way for the community to support the caregiver. Note that online crowdfunding platforms can sometimes be a challenge to retrieve money from in a timely manner—old-fashioned checks, cash, or instant app transfers can be a better option.

You might ask several friends to assist with the tasks above so that no one gets too overwhelmed. In an ideal world, the entire village would come together to care for the one who is dying, but this isn't always possible. Try to make do with what you have. I am part of a group of nearly a dozen women who care for an elderly man living alone in his remote home. We take turns caring for him in rotation, one week at a time. We are a team, but we also care for him individually in our own ways.

🌿 Herbal Support

When preparing the protective shell, a large pot of rosemary at your front doorstep or just inside will help safeguard your home energetically. A large bunch of fresh eucalyptus can also be nice.

📍 Alternative Location

In a hospital or nursing home, the outer and inner worlds are in much closer proximity. A designated person can oftentimes (casually) stand guard in the room or outside in the lobby of an ICU. This person can be the energetic buffer, asking people to lower their voices if the visiting crowd becomes rowdy.

Smoke Ceremony to Seal the Outer Nest

This simple incense/smoking/smudging ceremony simply demarks the boundary between that which is the outside world and what is now the inside world. Smoke ceremonies have been performed throughout time and around the world for a variety of reasons and intentions, including energetic cleansing, food preparation, meditation, offerings to deities, spell work, and spirit communication. Smoke ceremonies can be done with herbs in wrapped bundles (as in the instructions below) or herbs that are chopped and crushed to be placed on a stone or in a shell over hot charcoal.

1. Retrieve a hefty bunch of dried culinary sage, pine, juniper, yarrow, mugwort, Saint John's wort, cedar, thyme, rosemary, lavender, or any combination of these and wrap them tightly into a bundle. Look for what grows locally and is not a threatened plant.*

2. Light your herb bundle over a flameproof bowl until a small flame has caught. The idea for this ceremony is that it is quite smoky, to signify a cleansing and protective barrier around the house, apartment, or tent—wherever your loved one is dying. With your bowl of smoking herbs in hand, walk in a circle around the perimeter of the environment where your loved one is dying. Complete the circle by ending in the place where you began.

3. Remember to state your intention and hold that intention throughout the entire demarking. An intention may be something like this: *May only tranquility and genuine loving intention pass this threshold.*

Unscented Protective Sprays

Protective sprays can be used for the caregiver or the one dying—or both. Choose protective sprays for each individual based on what you believe is needed. Some people use the word "luck" instead of protection. For example, one person might wear a lucky bracelet to keep them safe, another person might wear a protection bracelet to keep them safe. These protective sprays hold the same idea, but be sure to state your intention clearly when making and using the spray.

---

*Culinary sage works very well. Please do not use white sage, which is a threatened plant and should be reserved for First Nations and Native American people.

When scent sensitivities exist or if your loved one is in the ICU or a similar location where scents are not allowed, these scentless protectors are wonderful. (You'll find more on how to be scent-free in chapter 3.)

1. Create a statement to repeat (in Sanskrit this is called a *mantra*) throughout the selection of materials and preparation of the spray. Intention is everything. A protective intention might be: *Ease of transition out of life, free from mental, physical, emotional, and spiritual obstacles.*
2. Add small pieces of rose quartz, amethyst, or amber to the bottom of a clean, unused spray bottle and fill it with water from a favorite spot in nature. Cap and label the bottle.
3. If you sense fear or agitation arising from your loved one, spray around the room or on each corner of the bed while reciting your protective intention. (Do not spray at your loved one.)

Each place that I travel around the world I collect water and sometimes a bit of earth. When I make protective sprays, I like to add a bit of water from Machu Picchu in Peru, Cascada de Las Animas in Chile, or the Hill of Tara in Ireland. Of course, you can add any water you'd like from a place that holds great meaning for you. It could be from a stream or lake right by your house! Similarly, the most precious stones you know of may be found in your favorite spot by that stream. Love, clarity, and intention are everything in this activity.

PREPARING THE INNER NEST

The room I am imagining is modest, with one window, a bed, one chair, a lamp, and a side table. Throughout this book, you'll find suggestions for additional items you may wish to have on hand. However, around the world, even where resources are very limited, families still care for their dying loved ones at home. We make do with what we have and adjust to changing circumstances.

The inner nest is an intermingling of the practical and mundane and the intimate, ambient wishes of the one dying. Since this is so unique to each individual's preferences and each given situation, a logbook or journal for all to reference is helpful.

If the one dying is receiving hospice care, there will be a binder nearby for hospice and volunteer communication. In addition, a more intimate correspondence for the caregivers can be an invaluable resource for keeping everyone up to date (even up to the hour) on the changes that are occurring. Things like records of bedding changes, urination, bowel movements, and meds given (which should also be logged in whatever medical log you have been asked to use) along with notes like NO MORE VISITORS AT THIS TIME all can be logged in a family journal. This can also be a place for more intimate, keepsake notes. You might write down the names of visitors who stopped by or poems that were read, or record dreams or phrases the dying one has been using.

🌿 Herbal Support

Live plants in a room where someone is dying can be lovely and refreshing. They can be a reminder of the life cycle and the vibrancy, growth, and strength that remains even while death is active. Small seedlings in the room can be beneficial, as regular visitors watch the progress of growth during this time. This can also be a way to welcome and encourage children to visit: "Let's check on Grandma and see how the little marigolds are doing!"

Bouquets of greens or flowers radiate healing color and their own individual virtues. Fresh plants also absorb energy, so it's best to replace a bouquet when it looks spent (and return it to the earth instead of the garbage, if possible).

. . . .

Considering the Ecosystem and Permaculture Principles of Dying

Permaculture is a set of design principles based on whole-systems thinking, meant to easily incorporate the new into an existing system with the least amount of impact to the environment. This was originally created with agriculture in mind by Australians Bill Mollison and David Holmgren. I like to apply permaculture principles when contemplating the environment of the one who is dying. This can be an interesting and helpful way to create and/or reveal the space one would feel comfortable dying in.

First, observe the outside environment. Try to look at it from above. Depending on your location, this may mean using your imagination to reason out the location of things, using a drone for an outside aerial view, climbing stairs, or looking out the window from an adjacent building. Draw a map of the outside landscape. Is there a dangerous front step that visitors should be aware of? Which room receives the morning or afternoon sunlight? Which side of the building receives the most wind?

Observe the inside environment. Is it a busy household? What are the patterns of the inhabitants? Are they typically active at night? Morning? Are there moments of silence at a particular time each day or throughout the week? What resources are available? Where is the running water in relation to the one dying? What are the snags or dysfunctional behaviors of the house, or the inhabitants? (You do not necessarily need to change or fix these aspects, but it can be helpful to know where they are.) Dysfunction can look different to different people, and when it comes to working with a dying individual, we as caregivers and death doulas sometimes need only observe to gain empathy.

What is your role in this greater system? Allow your environment and activities to offer you feedback, then self-regulate. Did your energy level drop just after you ate? What did you eat that could've caused this? Do you just need a nap?

After you have fully observed the many nuances of the living and nonliving systems in the place where your loved one is dying, you can adapt to changes easily and implement remedies where needed. You will know that the toilet on the first floor should not be used during heavy rainstorms or that the children in the upstairs apartment always stampede up the stairs after school but are quiet after 7:00 p.m., so that is the best time for visitors. You may know that the neighbor goes to the post office three times a week and may be able to pick up mail for the one dying as well. Use the systems that exist; work with the environment in a harmonious way to find and create the greatest ease.

. . . .

Clean, Clear, and Cleanse

Free the room of clutter so that you (the caregiver) can move freely without tripping. Sweep all corners and under the bed, and wash the windows. Use natural cleaners and aromatherapy items. For instance, sweeping with pine or other aromatic boughs can be really wonderful. Avoid synthetic sprays, air fresheners, and petroleum-based candles. Just getting a good breeze rolling through the space can help flush out old or stagnant energy. Scent-free techniques for cleansing or moving energy in a noninvasive way include feather fans, clapping, drumming, and using a chime or bells.

Herbal Support

After cleansing, mist a favorite aromatherapy or flower essence spray on bed sheets to provide a nice scent and help gently disinfect the area. A drop of good-quality lavender essential oil on the pillow can leave a wonderful scent that lasts for hours. A small pouch of herbs, such as dried lavender, organic roses, mint, or tulsi, can be tucked in a pillow or placed at the bedside—simply rub the pouch between your hands to activate the scent.

Ceremonial Intention for the Inner Nest

You are creating a sacred space, a precious nest where the dying person can be held. A space where an individual will inhale and exhale their last breath. A space where a spirit or soul will exit a body. You are holding the energetic space for this transition as much as the room itself is sheltering you from the elements outside.

Actively engaging in this energetic work is sometimes referred to as "holding space." This means that you do not cling to any one scenario but hold the intention of keeping your mind open and calm, free from negative or positive thoughts, desires, or beliefs; you're holding a neutral zone for the unfolding of what transpires. In this open and held space, a great deal of feelings and emotions can come and go, rise and fall—and instead of having a sticky quality where they impact you or the one dying, they simply move through like a passing cloud. American Tibetan Buddhist teacher Pema Chödron says of emotions, "You are the sky. Everything else—it's just the weather." You can apply that to this work by holding a calm and spacious sky around you and the one dying as various weather systems (or visitors) move through.

Preparing the room energetically and carrying out proper cleansing will help you to boost your own immune system and ready your psyche for what will transpire. Hopefully the environment you prepare will be soothing to both you and the one dying, and to all who enter the inner nest.

Remember, though, that this individual will die with or without your efforts—and they will die on their own, in their own way. You can prepare thoughtfully for one of the most sacred acts in our human existence and also completely let it go. There is nothing to cling to and no certain way in which this will go.

ം∗ঞ

MINDFULNESS PRACTICE
Letting Go

Take a strong and soft stance. Imagine your feet plunging hundreds of miles down through the earth and a beam of light extending hundreds of miles into the sky. Look around you with clear, open eyes. Feel the breath rise and fall in your lungs. Your heart is beating. You are alive. Realize where you are and what you are doing. Close your eyes and let your thoughts expand beyond any of the known. In your humanness, you cannot ever fully know the significance or importance of the role that you play here on earth or as a caregiver. Realize this and even let that go, as well.

A nice statement of intention: *May this sacred space of transition remain safe, and in pure and eternal love.*

📍 Alternative Location

Ceremonies and rituals can be done anywhere. You can use a scentless protective spray to cleanse the room and a little bowl of salt can be used to absorb negative energies. When you feel the salt has done its job, disperse it outside (spreading it so that it won't harm the grass or plants).

CAREGIVING'S INNER CIRCLE

During active dying, an inner circle will develop. Those who are in closest contact with the one dying are not always blood relatives, and not everyone may approve of those who are present in the inner circle. Maybe this is the way it has always been, or maybe this inner circle of people is a new development due to estranged relationships, emotional preferences, or issues with travel and distance. Emotions run high and confusion is rife in times of stress—and dying is no exception. It can bring out the absolute glowing best in people, or great anger, frustration, and denial.

There is a delicate balance between making sure you say what you need to say and stepping back so that the situation can unfold with the most ease. There can be a lot of "I" talk: "I think this," "I have been there for this," "I'm the only one who should be doing this." Every situation is unique, so there isn't one quick solution. Try to keep listening, remain curious, and try to recognize the situation for what it is: the situation of a person dying. You, too, will experience this one day. Let the way you handle yourself and others during this particular death be the way that you hope others will handle themselves at the time of your own death. (More on this in chapter 6.)

SECRET NESTING

Note the secret nest that is forming. As I write this, I think of my father—an incredible healer and therapist who teaches self-love as if it is an art that no one can actually live without. He is right, of course. He speaks of an inner chamber of self-love, which I picture as a comforting nest. This is what is beginning to form within the heart of the one who is dying. Outside comforts begin to mean very little; and indeed, eventually they mean nothing at all as death moves closer and life moves away. I have found this kind of self-soothing most obvious in cats that purr while dying, or animals that go off by themselves to die and return to the comfort of a protective fetal position. In this position, the body can remember the comfort of the womb, the time before life outside.

This secret nest might be easily formed for some people—a short journey inward to find the final comfort to ease their transition out of life. For others, discovering and accepting entry to this inner chamber might mean finally giving in or letting go—which they may be too frightened or unwilling to do. At times, the external circumstances can be a hindrance. One gentleman I worked with was distraught that he was spending his last days in the ICU when he desperately wished to be at home in the nest he had been preparing for his dying days. I visited him in the hospital and as he was explaining to me that his nest was at home waiting for him, I gently reminded him that the nest that needed the most attention right now was the one inside of him. It did not feel good to say this, but he trusted me to be honest and I was not sure if he would make it home before his death. Tears flooded his eyes, but he nodded in understanding.

The secret nest is a place that is highly individual (and our cultural beliefs play a role), but our ego, our sense of self, is the only thing preventing us from understanding the universal Oneness that we all are. We cannot assist another on this journey inward before the great release, but we can remind the one who is dying that the journey is safe, that they are loved and that they will soon merge with love itself.

At age nineteen I gave birth to my first child. I entered the pushing stages but had to lie on my left side to alleviate pressure on my vagus nerve. I'd just had a hellish experience in the bathroom where my midwife needed to pull half of my cervix over the baby's head in order to allow passage out. Exhausted, unmedicated, and really starting to lose focus, I decided to let go. I had a strong foundation in meditation from childhood, and with total, blissful release, I went deep into my heart and made a conscious decision to abandon all hope of fruition. I thought to myself, *I might die, and that's okay.*

A quote attributed to Anaïs Nin reminds me of this inner work I was doing: "The day came when the risk to remain tight in a bud was more painful than the risk it took to blossom." With no pain, total relaxation, and engulfed in a white light so bright that I could not see a thing, my baby was born. After, when I asked why the lights had been turned on so bright (when my birth plan clearly stated my wish to have no overhead lights), my mother replied, "No, sweetheart. It was pitch black in there. Your midwife was using a dimmed headlamp."

I'm sharing this because, wherever I was, pain did not exist once I entered into total surrender. The white light was a harmonious merging with all of space and time. I went there, at will, into my own inner chamber and secret nest when the external circumstances became too much to bear. No, I did not die. But if death is anything similar to that welcoming simplicity, none of us have anything to worry about.

WEATHERING OUR DYING

We contend with weather all our lives, and it continues to play a role in our deaths. As your loved one now dies, what is the weather like? In what phase is the moon? Is it humid or dry? Is the electricity steady, flickering, or out?

In life, we endure storms of various kinds depending on where we live. Some of us have been terrified by tornadoes, hurricanes, fires, and ice storms. However, these storms are part of our natural world. If and when we can surrender to something that powerful (when we are so powerless), it can almost be comforting. Death can be like this.

I have often thought that more people should die in less traditional places. If you have a care system that can travel with you, and you have spent all your best days on the shores of your private beach, why not set up a bed and die there? If you have the care and the ability and have spent the best hours of your life in the forest, why not die in a bed there? I would love to be bedside at a forest death.

We can revel in the smell of rain on the earth or on hot pavement in the city, the scent of freshly mown fields in the country or the sight of cedar boughs weighed down by snow. We can savor the experience of sitting by a crackling fire that captivates our eyes, our nose, our skin. Enjoy the summer lilacs in bloom or fruit fermenting on the ground—whether apples, mangos, or lemons. Pay attention to bird song, crickets or peepers chirping at night, howls from animals in the wild, rushing rivers, the pounding waves of the ocean, or hot, steamy air. The most beautiful sensations might be enjoyed simply by opening a window.

Alternative Location

Windows or access to the natural world may not always be readily available. A nature film or recorded sounds of crickets or ocean waves might be helpful in these situations. Some children's night lights cast stars or rainbows around the room, or you can find grown-up versions made of rice paper that gently rotate to cast a soft light reminiscent of the dancing shadows of leaves.

Three
Dying Is a Sensory Experience

Our real reality is beyond the five senses.

Deepak Chopra

While the five senses may not all be available to a person (due to neuropathy, radiation, chemotherapy, injuries, and so forth), they can be a multidimensional exploration that can bring comfort. In addition, sixth sense activity may occur, and perhaps out-of-body experiences and sensations that we, the living, are unable to comprehend or even recognize.

HEARING

How we use our voice—the tone, speed, volume, and enunciation—makes a big difference in how our messages are received.

Much can be learned from how Fred Rogers (of *Mister Rogers' Neighborhood*) spoke. Whether he was speaking to a small child or a group of graduating college students, he spoke clearly, calmly, and intentionally. He seemed curious about how others spoke and tried to understand their way of speaking. This style of speech may be appreciated by those who process the spoken word more slowly, such as those who speak another language, who are hard of hearing, or who have slower processing. The same applies to individuals who are numb, disoriented, or overwhelmed with emotion (which is common among those who are dying or those who have just received news of a death).

Hearing is often the last sense to shut down as the transition out of life nears. Take great care to ensure that the only words spoken in the room are those intended for your loved one to hear. Because hearing often remains an active sense in the late stages of dying, a decision can be made whether to leave hearing aids in or take them out. Arguments should be taken out of the room, preferably out of the building.

This is a good time for apologies, I-love-yous, and saying anything that should have been said a long time ago. While these things can be said after the individual has died, such communication during life can be soothing to the one who is dying and comforting for the one moved to speak.

One very hard gift to give is permission for your loved one to die. Oh, yes, they will die no matter what. However, in many instances, when someone is given permission from their loved ones—if they are told it is okay, that they, the loved ones, will be okay—the person often dies soon after. This takes great courage from the living, and may not always be offered to the one dying for any number of reasons. (Anger, for instance, and difficult emotions, which are addressed in chapter 6.) This is okay, too.

Sounds In and Around the Room

Hearing is an integral part of the dying process. If the one dying is capable of hearing (with our without hearing aids) this is an important sense to tend to. Though your loved one may not respond in a way that you can recognize, sound plays a significant role when so many other senses may be dulled or no longer actively engaged. Those dying may no longer be able to enjoy the tastes of their favorite foods, they may have their eyes closed for much of the time, or they may have a pain in their body and prefer not to think about bodily sensations. This can be a wonderful time to enhance or soothe by sound.

- When resting, does your loved one prefer silence or soothing background noise such as a gentle fountain, music, or a crackling fire?
- Does your loved one have favorite books, poems, prayers, or sacred passages that could be recited?
- Does your loved one enjoy being sung to or is there favorite music they may wish to hear?
- Family members laughing and telling stories of past events can be really wonderful. The sounds of children playing can be a blessing as well.
- Natural sounds of the outdoors day or night can provide great comfort. At other times, closing doors and windows to quiet the space is the right thing to do.

Be aware of sounds that may be overwhelming or invasive. If someone is mowing the lawn outside, perhaps close the window. During active phases of dying, these kinds of sounds might not have any impact on the individual (or the household noises may be comforting). If the person is unable to communicate, observe them and use your intuition.

If your loved one is accustomed to television in the background or prefers zoning out on a smartphone, that might be all they want to do while dying as well. We may be seeing more of this kind of dying in our future. People rarely make 180-degree turns in preferences when they are on their deathbed. Not always because they don't wish for something different—sometimes it is a default to do what has always been done.

📍 Alternative Location

Sounds in hospitals and nursing homes can be highly invasive, especially if the one who is dying is in an emergency room or sharing a room. To help remedy this, aim to get very, very small. Make the space around your loved one extremely intimate. Draw the room divider curtains, sit close, whisper in your loved one's ear, and, if appropriate, use noise-canceling headphones either to create silence or to play their favorite music. Whether at home or in a hospital room, music can drown out unpleasant or unwanted noise and create a comforting sound space.

🌿 Herbal Support

Earaches can be soothed by gently rubbing from ear to shoulder in downward strokes. A warm, gentle mixture of mullein flower oil in or around the ear will soothe. Harvest or purchase ½ cup of freshly opened yellow mullein flowers and cover them with olive oil. Set the jar (lidded) in the hot sun for one to three weeks to let the sun's heat naturally draw out the medicine of the mullein flower. Strain the mixture and bottle it. It is now ready to use, and you will only need a couple drops at a time.

SMELL

Scent can be used to aid the comfort of one dying. How incredible when we catch a whiff of something and are suddenly transported back to a childhood holiday party we may hardly remember—but the scent brings us there in a nanosecond. (Of course, this can be for better or worse!) Because so many scents are new when we are children, they make a lasting first impression.

When I was writing this I asked some of my closest and oldest friends what scents remind them of comfort and love. It quickly became a sentimental discussion. One friend said the scent of lilac reminds her of hiding with her brother under the lilac trees with her treasured childhood corgis. Another said the smell of the sugar shack in spring and steam rolling out of the maple syrup pans reminds her of sugaring with her parents when she was little. My husband, Pablo, loves the scent of magnolia; it reminds him of strolling through Central Park in New York City with his father when the magnolia trees were in full bloom. For me, the scent of fresh hay and horse saddles reminds me of playing in my barn as a child.

Is your loved one comforted by particular scents or sensitive to smells? (Scent sensitivities are acknowledged in the next section.) Check to see if this is listed in a death plan. If there is no documentation of this and if the one dying is unable to communicate, you can try to discern the person's preferences by asking family members or close friends. Even if the dying person does not like essential oils or human-produced scents, there are many smells that can bring comfort.

- Is there an old shirt of a beloved that smells like them that can be draped across the one dying? Even if they are very far away, this can be shipped to the one dying to inspire feelings of safety and loving comfort.
- A friend of mine said a particular scented soap was comforting for her family. They kept going to the store to retrieve bars of the soap to put around the hospital room because it reminded them of their loved one who was dying.
- Go ahead and cook! Some of the most soothing smells come from fresh-baked cookies or simmering stews. Cooking might feel good for you, and for idle family or friends as well.
- A basket of freshly chopped herbs can smell sensational in a room.
- The scent of beeswax is hypnotic to my family because we have been candlemakers for so long. We swoon at the warm yellow glow and scent of a warm beeswax candle and feel instantly centered. (Beeswax candles also emit negative ions, which aid in air purification.)

There are thousands of plant-based scents out there! Invigorating smells might only be appropriate for the caregiver; they can be useful if you are feeling drowsy at a time when you need to be alert. Invigorating scents include cinnamon, mint, citrus, and eucalyptus. Some soothing scents are lavender, vanilla, frankincense, vetiver, and rose. Those are just a few of the easiest-to-find essential oils that are generally regarded as pleasurable among many cultures.

Alternative Location

Some hospitals and nursing homes are fine with scents, some are not. Ask what is possible. Perhaps remind those in charge that there are already many strong scents and chemicals in the room, so the scent of rose really shouldn't hurt anything.

Herbal Support

It's easy to make your own vanilla to use as a delicious aromatherapy spray (or to cook with). Fill a quart-size mason jar with vodka (any inexpensive brand will do) and add two or three whole vanilla beans. Secure the lid tightly and set in a cabinet for one moon cycle, shaking a couple of times per week. This will create the most delicious smelling (and tasting) vanilla extract. This mixture will not go bad. As you use up the extract, continue adding more vodka and more vanilla beans. To make the spray, dilute the vanilla extract with distilled water (¼ part vanilla extract and ¾ part water), and put it in a labeled spray bottle. Bonus: When the old vanilla beans are spent, remove them from the jar and compost the pods—but not before removing the seeds, which can be added to coffee or ice cream as a treat.

How to Be Scent-Free

Some individuals are sensitive to scents their entire life, and some develop scent sensitivities over time for a variety of reasons. This is true for those who are dying. Chemotherapy may cause this, but some dying people feel extremely nauseous simply because their body is changing. One woman I cared for did not talk for three days because almost any activity or any scent would cause her to feel like she needed to vomit. A hospice nurse arrived wearing perfume and my client had to send her away. The nurse had been asked not to wear any scents, but her jacket still carried the smell of the perfume. Something that might seem innocuous to you may be overwhelming to someone with scent sensitivities. This can include natural scents such as foods and essential oils, and unexpected ones such as the coffee you carry into the room with you. Even hugging someone wearing perfume can transfer the scent to you.

Common scents to watch out for include essential oils, soaps, dryer sheets, shampoos, deodorants, car "scent trees," cleaning chemicals, and cigarette smoke. When you are working with someone who has scent sensitivities, the world as you know it changes. It's actually a wonderful exercise in opening to and becoming aware of your surroundings. We often look for things in our environment that are dangerous or uncomfortable, but rarely does that include scent.

Look for unscented shampoos, conditioners, deodorants, creams, soaps, and detergents. Read the labels carefully and, if possible, try to open the cap in order to smell the product. Let your clothes sun-dry (as dryers can hold the scent of previously used dryer sheets). Be sure not to add any scents to a humidifier in your own room or in the space of the one dying.

When Scents from the Dying Are Unpleasant

Remember to remove soiled bedding, used bandages, the contents from flushing a surgical drain, and garbage from the room frequently to cut down on disturbing smells. If there are no sensitivities, you can also mask unpleasant scents with incense, essential oil diffusers, sage, lotions, and sprays. However, sometimes these external remedies can feel invasive to the one who is dying.

Foul smells can emanate from within the cavity of the body, open sores, or the mouth. If you feel discomfort or nausea due to smells while working with the one who is dying, try mouth breathing or sucking on a mint while in close contact.

Mouth Care

When a person's body is in the midst of the dying process, teeth-brushing will not be a top priority; comfort will take the lead. Hygiene can still take place but often without a toothbrush, strong toothpaste, and a sink. Instead you can use a mouth rinse (and perhaps a gentle balm if their lips are dry or cracked).

If the one dying has false teeth, a decision can be made whether or not to take them out. Although visitors might not be used to seeing the person without their teeth in, it might be more relaxing for the one dying not to worry about glue (and the caregiver not to have to worry about bacterial build up).

🌿 Herbal Support

Squeeze the juice from a slice of lime and combine with 1 tablespoon of honey in 1 cup of warm water. Stir or shake to dissolve. Use a swab or a small, smooth washcloth to cleanse the teeth, tongue, and mouth. The person may or may not be able to spit and swallow, so take care with the amount of fluid you use to avoid aspiration. In place of lime, lemon or mint can also be used. Honey is nice as it is both sweet and has antibacterial properties. Mint tea is another alternative. Mint is generally a pleasant, familiar flavor, since many toothpastes are minty.

TASTE

Depending on the phase of dying, your loved one may want small bits of food, a milkshake, smoothie, thickened liquid, only clear liquids, or nothing at all. The broth of favorite stews and clear liquid soups can feel nourishing and soothing. Ice cube chips can be helpful, and you can crush and squeeze the juice from blueberries or an orange to add to the cubes.

As vibrant living beings, we feel comforted by food and eating. We all have different diets and ideas of what is healthy or appropriate, but in general we feel better when we eat. For this reason, it can be uncomfortable for the healthy and vibrant to see their loved one either not able to eat or choosing not to. The same goes for drinking. We often think that even if we cannot eat, we should still hydrate. However, dehydration actually offers a kind of pain relief after the initial thirst subsides. An analgesic effect takes place with dehydration that can stimulate a kind of euphoria and pleasing lightheadedness.

It's okay if your loved one chooses not to eat or drink, and we need to honor this decision. In the medical world this is known as "voluntary stopping of eating and drinking" (VSED). A young boy in a family I worked with was proud to have picked fresh raspberries to give to his dying father—they were his favorite. However, eating was no longer an option for the father (whether due to nausea or a desire not to eat). In moments like that, a shrine offering is a nice way for the one dying to accept a precious gift. Even if they are not awake or able to accept the offering, it can be added to the shrine as a remembrance of their love of raspberries.

Animals that are dying stop eating and eventually stop drinking as well. This is natural. It is not important to push healthy foods and hydration at this point, but we can be sure to eat and stay hydrated ourselves—in fact, this is vital for caregivers.

Whatever the dying person's intake situation, if all they are craving is chocolate frosting—well, doesn't that sound delightful? This phase of life is not about maintaining physical health, it is about soothing and letting go.

Alternative Location

Use a portable cooler to bring your own specially prepared ice cube chips or homemade broths.

Herbal Support

Although your loved one may not be eating or drinking, they may appreciate a gentle CBD salve to soothe their lips (see recipe on page 56). A scent can be added such as orange or mint to inspire the aromatic pleasures of eating something fresh and familiar. You can obtain CBD online or from an organic farmer in your area. This salve can be used for a great many things as it helps to reduce pain and inflammation and has antibacterial and antifungal properties. When my father-in-law had terribly cracked feet through his chemo and radiation treatments, this salve helped greatly. He also enjoyed having his feet rubbed.

Healing CBD and/or Calendula Oil

For this recipe you will need a double boiler and cheesecloth along with the following ingredients. The quantities are just suggestions and can be adjusted depending on how dense you wish the oil to be. Remember that coconut oil changes consistency with temperature.

¼ to ½ ounce CBD flower

⅛ ounce (or less) calendula flower

1 cup coconut oil or olive oil

Several drops orange, mint, rose, or lavender essential oil (optional)

Start by heating the crumbled CBD in a 230°F oven for approximately forty minutes. (This heating process is called decarboxylation.) After this, chop the heated buds until they are crumbly.

In a double boiler with gently simmering water in the bottom pot, add the crushed CBD to the top pot and top with the oil so that it is completely covering all of the buds. (If you would like the CBD content to be less potent, add more oil.) This is a very slow extraction and will be left on the stovetop for a couple of hours. Keep checking the water level and ensure that it gently simmers but doesn't become a rapid boil.

Options! You can add the calendula flowers to the top of the double boiler at the same time as the CBD or you can prepare the calendula separately (with the same double-boiler method described just above). By mixing them or keeping them separate you can create different oil variations.

After two hours, remove from heat and use cheesecloth to strain the herbs out of the oil. The oil will be hot so take care in straining the mixture. (I use a heat-resistant silicone oven mitt.) The herbs left after straining the oil can be added to a therapeutic bath; be sure to keep them in the cheesecloth pouch or put a drain-strainer in the tub to avoid clogging the pipes!

If you desire a scent, add several drops of therapeutic-grade essential oil, such as rose or lavender.

The color of this oil will range from green to very dark green depending on the potency of the CBD. This beautiful healing and soothing oil can be used as a base for many different applications. You can keep it in its concentrated form—to use on sore muscles, aid sleep, or reduce other inflammation—or dilute it with more oil for massage.

SIGHT

What we value as a soothing sight varies from person to person. Most of the time, familiar surroundings are soothing. Plants, crystals, salt lamps, silks, and images of nature can be soothing—but if these aren't familiar to the one who is dying, the person may end up feeling uncomfortable.

An effort should be made to create a visually pleasant environment in the room. For instance, try not to have too many medical items within your loved one's gaze, if possible. It's easy to put medicines in a basket and cover it with a pretty cloth. Maybe store charts flat rather than hanging them on the wall to be seen by all.

Here are some things that I have found helpful to consider when working with those who are in the tender phases of making peace with their visual surroundings.

➣ Are there certain images that soothe your loved one? Consider moving favorite artwork closer to the one who is dying.

➣ Photos of loved ones on a nearby table can be comforting for the dying one to view. My friend Salicrow, a psychic medium and author, explains that adding photos of ancestors in particular can be helpful. This might include pictures of deceased parents, friends, or children. With these images as a focus, the one dying is encouraged to go *toward* these loved ones. Viewing photos of the living, the ones who will be missed here on earth, can instead anchor the dying person here.

➣ Shadow play on the walls and ceiling can be soothing. Sometimes the sun will filter through a tree waving in the breeze or through a lace curtain and cast shimmers or shadows around the room. Suncatchers and hanging crystals that cast rainbows around the room can be beautiful.

➣ Does the person dying prefer their space light or dark? A blackout curtain or a heavy blanket over the window can help if darkness is preferred. When needed, use candles (real or LED), dimmable lights, or a handheld light to assist and work around the individual. If you must use overhead lights periodically, give warning to your loved one before you turn on the switch. A soft eye mask could be helpful if the room needs to be heavily lit and it feels disruptive.

➣ Some may enjoy a dimly lit room with twinkle lights or candles (even solar-charged or LED). Of course, it's worth mentioning that people who are dying spend a lot of time with their eyes closed, so this ambiance might be more for the sake of the caregivers or those visiting.

- Personally, I love sleeping in a beam of sunlight. I added this to my death plan so that no one closes the shades.
- Bouquets of flowers can be wonderful, though they are not always allowed in all hospital wings.

🌿 Herbal Support

Warm bags of chamomile are very nice for sore or tired eyes. This works whether you harvest your own fresh chamomile flowers to make a tea or use organic pre-bagged tea from a store. Simply brew a cup of tea, wait for it to cool until it is a temperature that feels good, and either place tea-soaked cloths over the closed eyes or put the tea bags directly onto the closed eyes.

TOUCH

The dying body is going through a process not unlike the discomfort of coming through the birth canal. Understand that your touches are the last ones this individual will experience in their life. Touch may be soothing or painful. Do your best to be gentle and mindful while doing what must be done to physically care for your loved one.

- First, determine if the one dying is accustomed to touch or if they have rarely been touched in their life. It is appropriate to ask to touch or tell the person that you are about to touch them before you offer assistance.
- Does your loved one find comfort in hand-holding or a gentle head or foot massage? You may use lightly scented oils

to gently rub hands, feet, temples, and shoulders. This can be extremely comforting. Be sure that your hands are warm and that the room is warm enough for whichever part of the body you are exposing for massage.

❧ Note that dehydration can make touch painful. So, in this instance, massage would be extremely gentle or not at all. Hand-holding, forehead kisses, and kind whispers of love are almost always appropriate.

After your loved one has departed, you may still wish to wash their hands and face, comb their hair, hold their hand, kiss them, or even lie down next to them. The wish to touch—or avoid touching—the dying and the dead is unique to each individual.

At the home funeral of my father-in-law, my three-year-old daughter was invited to touch her deceased grandfather. She chose not to but instead played close beside him during the time that his body was there. She decorated him with crystals, placed flowers around him, straightened his blanket, and cared for his body while never touching him.

⊙ Alternative Location

You can touch your loved one in nearly every situation. To add the feel of something familiar, you may wish to bring a blanket from their home for their bed.

Four

What the Physical Body Does during the Dying Process

Dying is enormously hard. The labor of it—and it is labor, of the same kind as that which brings life into the world—is relentless, demanding.

STEPHEN JENKINSON, *DIE WISE*

The elements of earth, wind, fire, and water in the dying body tremble, inflate, crackle, and flow . . . and little by little they cease to be active. There is a pause during this time when the life is ending, and the death is beginning. This precious time is space where the crossing over is happening. After death, the play of elements once again starts up and the ecology of death begins. There is much activity in dying, even when the individual is lying still in bed.

ACHES AND PAINS

As the body's systems begin to slow and cease to operate, certain pains arise and then fade. What might be painful in one moment may not be painful in the next. The pain may also endure. Assure your loved one that this is perfectly natural and offer encouragement, medicinal support, and Reiki or other noninvasive body work, if possible. Your loved one may moan and act agitated. This is all normal. Imagine a mother in deep, deep labor, or imagine the earth as it shifts and groans beneath the surface.

We all want to help alleviate pain and we should do the best we can. While many people find herbal supports helpful in this area, many dying people choose to take pain medication as well. Integrative medicine is wonderful. If your loved one receives hospice care, pain relievers will be easy to obtain. Discuss with the doctor the appropriate amount of sedation and medications (and refer to relevant notes in the dying person's death plan whenever possible). Honor the wishes of your loved one and follow your intuition.

Don't be embarrassed to ask about medicinal cannabis. THC often helps tremendously with end-of-life discomforts such as pain and nausea. Smoking is not the only way to experience the relief that THC offers, it can also be used topically or ingested. It can be eaten in sweets, used as butter, made into a lollipop or gummy, or taken with a dropper under the tongue. "Weed" is anything but a nuisance plant, and it's not just for hippies or rebellious youth! The non-psychoactive component of cannabis is called CBD and it has many of the same benefits. Some of the plant's terpenes (oils that give the plant its unique smell) have been known to assist with difficulties due to ulcers, arthritis, gastrointestinal problems, depression, muscle relief, and chronic pain. Different strains offer different medicinal supports. Ask a specialist to help you navigate the options.

✎ Herbal Support

Massage or gentle touch with a natural oil (such as olive, sesame, or coconut) infused with a drop or two of a favorite essential oil may be helpful in relieving pain and can ease fear and anxiety. First ask, "Would a massage feel nice?" If the answer is yes, you can start with either a hand or a foot and then move to the shoulders, neck, and head. Easy does it when massaging; use slow, even, gentle strokes.

You may wish to topically apply arnica or a camphor-menthol gel or cream to help relieve mild to medium soreness, pain, and inflammation. Be sure that anything with menthol does not touch any open wounds—and keep it away from eyes.

TEMPERATURE

As the human body shuts down, body temperature will fluctuate between hot and cold—a real weather system will move through, and it will not always be consistent in all parts of the body. Often, the element of fire will rise in the form of a fever, which will spike just before death. However, this occurrence does not necessarily mean that death is imminent.

In addition to temperature fluctuation, patches of skin may change color. Known as mottling, this often occurs as the circulatory system begins to shut down. Depending on skin color and the particular person, mottling may or may not be easily visible or happen at all.

❧ Herbal Support

A damp cloth (warm or cool) can be used on the forehead, feet, or hands. A couple drops of soothing essential oil (such as lavender, vanilla, frankincense, vetiver, or rose) can be added as desired. Dry, heated cloths or hot rice packs that contain dried fragrant herbs can also be useful (if you have a microwave available). Hot-water bottles can feel nice, but be sure they are not too hot. A thin towel between the hot-water bottle and the skin is appropriate. If you are placing the hot-water bottle on the individual, be sure it does not feel too heavy to them. If in doubt, simply place it alongside the person and adjust their body around it. Be sure not to leave a cold or lukewarm hot-water bottle on or near the person.

BREATHING AND HEART RATE

During active dying, the element of air plays a strong role. You may find yourself focusing on the dying person's intake of air, similar to the careful monitoring of parents watching their newborn baby.

Breathing may become shallow and rapid, or there may be long pauses with stillness between breaths. The same is true for the heart rate. The heart may beat very fast, or it may beat so gently that you cannot tell if it is still beating at all. This is normal. If the dying one seems to be paying attention to it, assure them that this is perfectly natural and that they are doing this just right. If they cannot breathe, stroke the top of their head rhythmically while focusing on your own breath. Soothe them with quiet words of encouragement.

It's quite common for a rattling noise to develop in the throat or chest. You may try to adjust your loved one's position by turning their head to the right or left or elevating their shoulders. In many cases this rattling may irritate the caregiver more than the one dying. If you believe your loved one is experiencing pain, discomfort, or irritation associated with this, you can ask a nurse or doctor how to help.

Sometimes the one dying begins to pull at their clothing or bedsheets. This is usually due to decreased oxygen and a feeling of restriction. You may be able to ride this out with them, but if it goes on for a long period of time and you believe it indicates anxiety, talk to the doctor or nurse.

When the breathing of the one dying is challenging, return to your own breath to center and calm yourself.

❧

MINDFULNESS PRACTICE
Returning to Your Breath

A basic meditation practice is simply to keep your conscious mind on your in-breath and your out-breath. I've provided two simple variations below; both of these tools can work beautifully in a situation where you need space, clarity, and time to separate from whatever thoughts are holding your mind hostage.

1. *Take a deep breath in. And let it all out. Take a few more slow, deep breaths before letting your breathing return to a more natural rhythm. Keep your mind on the in and out of your breath. When a thought enters your mind, pop it as if it*

*were a bubble or send it off in a cloud and keep following your
breath.*

2. *Breathe in pure, clear, calming energy. Exhale the stagnant,
   confused, stressed energy. And repeat.*

Alternative Location

Breathing, heart rate, temperature, and other bodily functions
are heavily monitored in an ICU. You will be able to watch
every digit go up or down, and a surge or plummet can send
your heart reeling. If you can, keep your gaze on the human
rather than the machines. They are meant for a medical realm—
not an emotional one. Perhaps imagine that the machines are
gauging the life story of the individual. There have been ups and
downs and some steady times, but nothing can actually monitor
the preciousness of the present moment.

EATING, DIGESTION, AND ELIMINATION

During dying the fire elements of digestion and water retention
and release intermingle sporadically in the body. Diarrhea, constipation, and nausea can be uncomfortable or even cause pain.
This can be related to certain medications, illnesses, or the body's
change in functioning.

If your loved one is incontinent, disposable or washable
adult diapers or underwear can be used. You may want to use
disposable wipes (like baby wipes) or soft washable cloths. Be
sure to use a clean part of the cloth for each wipe, and always
wash from the front perineal area back toward the anus. You

can roll the individual onto their side in order to remove or attach incontinence underwear or adult diapers. (See draw-sheet instructions in "Bedding and Lying in Bed," page 74.)

If you know the person is lying in wet undergarments and you see that this is causing irritation, alert your loved one and tell them you are going to assist with changing them so they can rest more easily. If they have been restless for a long period of time and have finally fallen asleep, you may not want to rush to change an absorbent undergarment.

If your loved one slows or stops eating, there will be fewer bowel movements, then less urine, and then little or none of either. If your loved one has a catheter, emptying the bag is eas-ily done. Ask the nurse to show you how to do this at home and how to clean the tubes and cleanse the person's perineal area.

Eliminating with others around can be humiliating and even difficult. (Think how long we have been trained to not wet or soil our pants.) Consider leaving the room so that the person's muscles can relax enough to let go. Other ways to help: turn on water or play a recording of ocean waves or a waterfall crashing.

This book is focused on bedridden care, but small transfers to a bedside commode can be done with enough support.

Herbal Support

A variety of herbal enemas can be taken to relieve constipation. However, you'll need to check with a doctor, as some—such as the coffee enema—might also increase heart rate due to the caf-feine. Chamomile is gentle. Red raspberry leaf, catnip, apple cider vinegar, or epsom salts can also work quite well. Be sure to use the correct dilution necessary for it to be effective and also gentle.

HANDWASHING

Handwashing and sanitizing is the best way to prevent the spread of germs and infection and keeps everything feeling fresh. A hand sanitizer can be kept by the doorway to the house or room, along the bedside, or in your travel bag. Not all alcohol-based sanitizers are strong enough to inactivate viruses; look for an alcohol content of at least 60 percent. However, virus-killing sanitizer is not always what is needed. Sometimes something more gentle will serve well.

MINDFULNESS PRACTICE
Mindful Cleansing

Handwashing is a time for *you*. This is an opportunity to look at your hardworking hands and to wash them lovingly, showing appreciation for their capabilities.

> *Take your time, being thankful for the water. Massage your palms, and use the opposite hand to push your fingers and wrists backward to stretch those ligaments. When you wash between your fingers and under your nails, envision cleaning out the forgotten pockets of your being. Send your stresses out through your fingertips, washing them away.*

🌿 Herbal Support
The following hand refresher recipe is easy to make. It is not intended for use as an antiviral. (The CDC recommends at least 60 percent ethyl alcohol for sanitizers intended to kill bacteria and viruses.)

Witch Hazel Hand Refresher

For this recipe you will need a 2-ounce spray bottle along with the following ingredients.

1 ounce witch hazel

½ ounce liquid aloe vera

½ ounce yarrow tincture, distilled water, or vodka

10 drops essential oil, such as Thieves blend, lavender, rosemary, lemon, red thyme, lemongrass, or eucalyptus

Mix ingredients in the spray bottle and shake well before each use.

Note: Be sure to check with the overseeing physician or medical staff about the proper safety protocol regarding caring for your loved one. In some instances it might be appropriate to wear masks and gloves or other personal protective equipment. At times, even if you are not advised to take specific health precautions, you may prefer to wear gloves when changing undergarments or flushing drainage tubes. It is always a good idea to wash your hands thoroughly with soap and water before and after you offer physical care. An inviting handwashing station is appropriate to set up in or outside of the room for visitors. A lovely station might include an antibacterial soap that does not have an overpowering scent, bundles of flowers nearby, and an herbal hand lotion. The more inviting the area, the more people will be delighted to visit it, which will reduce the spread of germs and viruses.

WOUND CARE

If the individual you are caring for has bandages, it is appropriate to continue changing them to keep the wound clean. Wound care materials (and disposable gloves, if you'd like) are available in drugstores and online.

Wounds should be cleaned gently from the inside out. It's important not to cringe or make faces when providing this care (unless that is your particular lighthearted relationship with the person). A sense of humor can be great, but be sure you're not making your loved one feel self-conscious or burdensome.

🌿 Herbal Support

Depending on the type of wound and how you clean it, the soothing aid you use on it will vary. A very gentle soapy water mixture or a saline solution can be used, as seawater is often healing. If you are making your own salt water, be sure to use distilled water (or boil tap water), and make sure the salt is fully dissolved in the water before using. A soothing calendula salve that contains antibacterial herbs such as lavender and yarrow will help minor scrapes and cuts but is not appropriate for deeper, oozing wounds. Remember that there may not be a tremendous amount of healing at this point, but cleanliness and soothing remain a priority.

SPONGE BATHING

Depending on the condition of your loved one's skin, bathing can be a sensitive and delicate undertaking. Elderly individuals, especially, have skin that is thin and can tear easily.

Bathing is not always welcomed enthusiastically by the one dying. It can often leave them exhausted and they may become easily chilled. In addition, bathing is a time of vulnerability, as parts of the naked body are exposed. For all of these reasons, it is vital that bath time be gentle and kind but also quite swift.

Explain to your loved one that it is time to bathe but that they do not need to do anything—not even get up out of bed! You will wash and dry each part of the body gently, and immediately cover them again with their sheet or blanket before moving on to the next part. In this way, they are never fully naked or fully wet.

1. First, warm the room as much as possible and gather your supplies. You will need several thick, absorbent bath towels, a few extra-soft washcloths, a clean set of clothes or pajamas for immediately after the bathing, a basin of gentle soapy water, and a separate bowl of clean water (both should be between 105–110°F).

2. When you are ready to begin, roll the individual onto one side and place towels beneath them. Then do the same on the other side. To maintain discretion and to keep the individual warm, only undress the part that you are washing at that time while keeping the rest of the body covered. This can be done in four segments. Begin with the top half of the person while keeping the bottom half dressed or completely covered. Wash and dry one arm and breast and half of the abdomen, while keeping the other arm and breast covered until you are ready to begin on that side. Repeat in the same way for the legs and feet.

3. Use an extra-soft washcloth to cleanse with gentle soapy water. Never apply soap directly to the skin or cloth; instead add the soap to the water and swish it around. Pat to wash and moisten. Then, with clean water drawn from a separate bowl, pat to rinse. With a dry washcloth, pat to fully dry. Do not rub or scrub. Be sure to clean areas of skin-against-skin such as armpits, creases under breasts, folds of stomach and thighs, the groin area, and between buttock cheeks. This is where bacteria tend to grow, and the area can begin to smell or develop a wound if not cleansed properly (or if adult absorbent underwear prevents the skin from breathing).

4. Once the bath is done and the person is dry, remove the damp towels from beneath them and dress them again.

While this book is focused on bedridden care, know that small transfers to a bedside commode for bathing time can be done with enough support. In this position, you may be able to use a handheld bidet, which releases more water at a time than sponge bathing. In this case, you would drape towels or blankets over the person's shoulders while you bathe them as they sit on the commode.

Wash and tend to feet carefully, cleaning and fully drying between the toes. In some cultures, this is a preparation for the journey ahead. Wrapping hands or feet in warm cloths that are aromatic or heated (or both) can be soothing between baths.

Herbal Support

Soak a few sprigs of rosemary, lavender, marigold, yarrow, chamomile, or any type of basil in the warm wash water. The scent can be wonderful for both caregiver and recipient. If the person has scent sensitivities, omit aromatic herbs. Nonaromatic cleansing herbs, such as calendula, violet, or chickweed, can be used instead. Be sure that no pieces of herbs or flowers end up on the washcloth.

For perineum care, pure rose water can be mixed into distilled water to clean this sensitive area. The distilled rose water mixture is mildly astringent and cleanses and nourishes the skin. Other distilled herbal waters (also known as floral water or hydrosols) can be used.

MOISTURIZING

Coconut oil is a great skin moisturizer in warmer climates or when warmed above room temperature (it's a solid that melts at about 77°F). In cooler climates, a calendula or CBD salve (see recipe on page 56) is a good option. Olive or sesame oil can be nice, but be sure not to leave your loved one too slippery. Do not moisturize between the toes.

BEDDING AND LYING IN BED

Pillows, sheets, and towels will become a caregiver's best friend. It might be a chore to keep the linens clean, but they can make all the difference in maintaining a sanitary and comfortable environment. Pillows for propping are helpful. Use a waterproof mattress cover and waterproof pillow protector, if possible.

To avoid having to change all bedding every time it is soiled, use two layers of sheets so that you can remove one layer easily and still have a fresh one underneath. You can also place disposable or washable absorbent pads beneath the dying person's bottom.

You will likely find it helpful to make up a drawsheet for under the trunk of your loved one's body. To do so, take a twin-size sheet and fold it in half (or in thirds) so that it fits only under the trunk of the body. With two people, each corner of the drawsheet can be gripped, which makes moving and rolling the person much easier. This works best if the one dying is in a twin-size or hospital bed. It is possible to add a drawsheet to larger beds, but it will require kneeling on the bed beside the person (which can be hard on your back).

A drawsheet can be used when changing soiled sheets, to move the person higher or lower in the bed, to roll them from side to side, and to change incontinence underwear. This maneuvering is at least a two-person job if you are working with an adult patient. If you are working with a very small adult or a child, it might take only one or two people. Be sure to smooth the sheets after adjusting, in order to prevent sores.

If the linen supply is limited and a drawsheet cannot be used, simply roll the individual back and forth with your hands to clean and change them. Eventually, though, they will either inch up or inch down in the bed, and a drawsheet will prevent you from having to hoist them up in a more physical way.

If the one who is dying is completely immobile, occasionally roll them gently from their back to their side, and a couple hours later roll them to the other side. It can be helpful to set a timer or reminder for some routine care tasks, as day and night blend into one another and time passes outside of ordinary reality.

Use pillows to cushion the dying person's limbs. I find four pillows helpful when they're lying on their side: one under the head, a second behind the back for support, one between the legs to prevent rubbing and support the hips, and one under the top arm (as if they are hugging a teddy bear). Four pillows are also helpful when lying on the back: one under the head, one under the knees, and one under each arm. This helps to support the entire frame and to prevent bedsores. A fifth pillow or a rolled small blanket can be used to lift the heels off the bed so they are not even touching the sheets. A lot of pressure lands on the heels when an individual is bedridden, and they can become extremely tender.

⚲ Alternative Location

Nursing staff in hospitals and nursing homes are experts at maintaining a clean, comfortable bed for the person in it. However, this doesn't mean you can't ask to assist if you'd like.

WHAT TO PACK IN A HOSPITAL BAG

Sometimes all your plans get thrown out the window and you find yourself unexpectedly in the hospital. The dying person may fall while out for a walk and the ambulance scoops them up, or an out-of-town relative who is legal next of kin decides that more care should be given or that the situation isn't right. These things happen. I've been an event coordinator for twenty years, so I like to prepare for plan B whenever possible.

Here are some suggestions for making an acute-care death feel a little more holistic. (Much of what is referenced here is explained elsewhere in the book.) Some of these things can be prepacked in a bag that can be easily grabbed for quick departure, while others you will add as needed.

For the One Dying
- Advance directive or living will
- Personal grooming kit
- Makeup and/or nail polish (if they wish for you to apply it for them)
- Bedspread from home (something small, lightweight, and washable)
- Salt and a bowl if you wish to do a ceremony to absorb negative energy
- Scentless protective spray
- Essential oils (if not against hospital policy)
- Specialty ice cubes (in a cooler) and perhaps homemade broths
- Salves, lip balms, moisturizers
- Massage oils
- Portable shrine (photos, special rocks, LED candle)
- An outfit and shoes to dress them in after they pass away

For the Caregiver
- Personal grooming kit and toiletries
- Change of clothes
- Comfortable shoes or slippers
- Your own medications and vitamins
- Favorite teas for soothing or invigorating
- Nonperishable snacks

- Spray bottle or drops of bitters to add to drinks to aid digestion
- Travel/neck-support pillow (in case you have to sleep sitting up)
- Book, puzzle, or something to relax your mind if you need a break
- Charger for your phone and other electronics

. . . .

Sweet Annie

I was blessed to work with a woman named Annie at the end of her life. Of course, I feel this with every person who welcomes me into their world in their most vulnerable last days on earth. But Annie modeled something for me that I had not yet witnessed.

In early July, Annie found out that she had stage 4 pancreatic cancer. Though she had previously had some general belly issues, she by no means thought she had terminal cancer. She was a very active teacher and was joyfully living her life (with her teaching calendar planned through the fall of the following year). After receiving this diagnosis, she took a few days to contemplate her situation and talk to friends. By July 13th, she had contacted me to ask about my work as a death doula, and she hired me four days later. She said with a smile, "We have a lot of work to do because I'm heading out of here."

We carefully went over my forty-page questionnaire and information booklet about dying, death, and disposition (a customized advance directive and ethical or living will), and over the following two weeks she read through each section, digesting it in her own time. She engaged with each segment of the booklet on her own and was able to write her own obituary, plan her funeral and memorial, and choose the method of disposition that best suited her lifestyle. That was it. Her end-of-life paperwork had been completed, her business had been sold, she said her good-byes, and even had a private goodbye party in her home.

I have never worked so quickly as a death doula to be sure everything was in order. Four weeks and 450 emails later, Annie lay peaceful and still in her bed at home, like a golden angel (or like the dandelions she loved so well).

This is the result of death nesting done well. Because she did not take time denying her dying, she weighed her options for disposition curiously and was able to become the first green burial in her local cemetery. As an herbalist, she fully understood the gift of life she was offering the earth with her body.

Not a single person could deny that Annie's exit was exquisitely graceful. Though she had no partner or children and her siblings lived out of state, she was surrounded by a community of caring, loving, conscientious human beings who cared about her and for her through the dying process (and continued with the arrangements that followed after death).

In my work, I am reminded often of the importance of death nesting as part of life. Dying as an unpartnered individual poses many challenges. You wonder how your body will be cared for after your death. Some people have become so capable living a single lifestyle that it can be difficult to accept the help of others. That said, there are plenty of people who are partnered and their partner dies first, or an unexpected separation or illness prevents that care from being a possibility.

We must care for each other. Just as it takes a village to raise a child, it takes a village to assist the dying. Just as we should practice death nesting personally in our daily lives, we should consider death nesting as an entire village so that we can be prepared to support one another.

· ·

Herbal Support from Annie

Even on her deathbed, Annie was teaching about herbs. Through her friend who channels an angel, Annie shared this information with her circle of friends and asked that it be passed on to a wider audience: When it is seen that death is approaching, take three parts echinacea tincture to five parts water, given in teaspoon-full doses hourly. The result is calming and helpful, even with strong pain relievers like morphine. Whether homeopathic or allopathic, echinacea will helpfully potentiate morphine without hastening death.

Five

Mind, Spirit, and Emotion in the Dying Process

Time makes us old. Eternity keeps us young.

MEISTER ECKHART

eelings of anxiety and fear are common as death nears. This is normal and expected. Assure your loved one that they are doing this just right. Encourage them to hold their own concerns gently, to share if they are willing, and to know that they are loved.

There is no way we can mend every broken heart, concern, or regret. If we flash back to the secret nesting that is happening, the dying person's life review is something that we as caregivers cannot partake in by simply organizing paperwork or reasoning things out with them. There are some areas we cannot touch. You can tell the individual that you will take care of their children or loved ones—a comforting offer; but what they are feeling is the loss of being able to do that themselves. It is not uncommon to miss feeling attractive or to miss sex. Some have managed their whole lives around being desired by others, and now the focus involves no one other than themselves. A hole can open, exposing feelings of loneliness and being left out. "The world will go on without me" is a painful statement, and there is no way that we as caregivers can deny that.

Although this is one of the most difficult pangs in the mental labor of dying, if one can breathe deeper and dissolve into that, it can become an orgasmic release. For the one who is dying, the you that you thought was you is about to merge with everything you have ever loved in a way that no pain can touch. This is a relevant contemplation for us caregivers to examine ourselves so that we can hold that comfort for the one who is dying.

Continued contemplations for the caregiver can be helpful for maintaining empathy for the one dying while also recognizing that this time will happen for each of us.

⚜

MINDFULNESS PRACTICE
Perimeter Practice

One contemplation you can do is called "Perimeter Practice." This is my own term and a meditation that I have adapted from a form of practice I was taught a decade ago in my Buddhist community. I unintentionally engaged in this form of self-soothing as a teenage mother. While all my friends were exploring the world, going to college and partying, I was at home singing to my tiny baby and trying to get my milk under control. I'm really glad social media was not a thing then; it might have heightened my feeling of being left out to see all the photos of my friends wildly living life. Or, I suppose the opposite could have been true—I might not have felt so alone because I could have connected with others who were young and had children. Either way, I'm glad it was not an option then, as that period was a time of tremendous growth for me.

The original practice in my Buddhist community was intended for those who must be on duty, or at work with responsibilities, while others are celebrating or at the place that you would rather be. However, I have also applied it to contemplating death. The point of the practice is to rest in the present moment, looking directly at and relaxing into your own experience, ultimately finding contentment with your own life and your own situation. Death can be perceived as the ultimate version of being left out, but that is only one perspective. When you are left out of one thing, you are incorporated into another. This can be deeply comforting.

This can be done as a new meditator, and it is a practice that you can continue for your entire life. I recommend doing this exercise periodically not only as a death nesting practice but also as a way to fully realize the preciousness of your own life. This exercise should also help you to empathize with the one who is dying; just be careful to never presume that you know what they are going through. This practice requires that you are very gentle with yourself, so you may want to review the Nesting Meditation on page 4 before you begin.

Begin by sitting in a space that feels comforting (or at least safe). Let your mind wander over everything in the world that you cherish most. Make a list. It can be people, places, things, feelings, inspirations, foods . . . all earthly delights.

Sit with the list and one by one touch upon what it feels like to lose these cherished delights. Think of them as being out of your reach while everyone else in the world gets to continue loving all of them. How does that feel? Be gentle, but feel deeply.

Practice this again and again—practice feeling outside the perimeter.

Having rested in the knowledge that you are or will be separated from the most cherished things in your life, you will begin to feel completely isolated and alone. But that aloneness is not desolation. It is not an empty void.

In fact, the next step is to bring to mind all that you are thankful for. The things you appreciate about your life—what you have learned, the experiences you have had, and the people you have loved—begin to balance the feeling of separation and loss.

After a while, you learn that you're just fine. Actually, you may be even happier with yourself and the world with this new perspective on life. You might find you do not crave as much of something as you did before, or that you have a greater appreciation for something that you love. You also realize that you don't need those things to be happy—or at least fine. You are fine, just like everyone else who has never really needed those things at all. Likewise, when you are dying, you will be fine . . . just like everyone else who has died before you.

SUGGESTIONS FOR MENTAL SOOTHING

Mental soothing can happen in many forms. It might feel good to talk about life events as they are unfolding. Some people find comfort in talking about ailments that others have instead of focusing on their own. Soothing can also happen with turning away from the painful challenges at hand. When working with someone, it can help to loosely define what is causing anguish and go from there. If it is hard to touch upon directly with a question such as, "What would feel good to do/see/talk about right now?," try coming at the investigation from another angle. For example, look for emotional cues when you ask them about a favorite childhood story or what kinds of activities their grandchild is taking interest in. Cracking open a window to let in bird song might lift the dying one's gaze and invite conversation about the kinds of birds in the trees. Here are some additional suggestions for mental soothing:

- Read aloud from favorite books or tell stories about good times in the past.
- Play favorite music. Perhaps upbeat music is called for to bring a smile, or maybe melancholy music is needed to produce healthy tears.
- Bring in a chaplain, death doula, or clergy person if that is what is called for.
- Cover or remove mirrors if the dying person prefers not to see their reflection. As we die, our appearance changes and our perception of our appearance changes. In addition, clinging to how we look and who we are is not particularly helpful when dying.
- Is there something the dying person needs to share with someone? Take notes and deliver messages. If desired, a

"timed-release" plan can be implemented (meaning the note will be delivered after the person has died).

» Does the dying person have any last wishes? Maybe a trip to India was what your loved one always wanted. With technology, one can travel far without leaving the bed. Watching a live cam in India or having a conversation with someone there might be possible! Turn on traditional Indian music or have someone play live in the room. Bring in a specially prepared chai or dish with aromatic rice, curry, and coconut milk. Even if the person is no longer eating, just the music and smells of the spices might make them feel that they got one step closer. Think creatively about what you have and what is possible.

» Are there pets that should be brought close? There is nothing like a fur body to bring comfort, if the animal is willing.

» Is the person concerned about what will be done with their body after death? Learn the disposition options in your state or province and ask your loved one what they prefer. Many people want to know what will be done with their body but are too afraid to talk about it.

» Would the dying person just like some time alone? Often, people take the opportunity to die when someone leaves the room. We can sense this in some instances and feel hesitant to leave them alone. Rest assured, each person dies in their own unique way, and we as caregivers need to make room for that.

» If your loved one is still drinking, a cup of warm milk (whatever kind of milk they prefer) and some back-rubbing can be soothing. I used this simple technique for elderly patients who were restless in the middle of the night during my overnight shifts at a residential care facility.

- ⁓ In some instances, redirection can be helpful and appropriate. This involves gently guiding the dying person's thoughts to something that creates comfort and peace of mind. You can ask, "Would a hand massage feel nice?" Or comment, "This photo of your mother is really lovely."
- ⁓ Hospice has allopathic medicines that can help with anxiety—ask the doctor.
- ⁓ Silence. Sometimes, just silence is the perfect thing.

🌿 Herbal Support

Lavender or another favorite essential oil can transform the moment and help a person feel more calm. Provide a long-lasting scent with aromatherapy room-spray or a dot of essential oil on the shirt collar or pillow (avoiding the eyes and mucous membranes).

Anything that promotes sleep is helpful, such as a couple drops of valerian root tincture, hops, or a full-spectrum CBD and/or THC extract under the tongue.

PSYCHEDELICS AND VIRTUAL REALITY

Indigenous cultures around the world have practiced healing rituals with psychedelic plants and fungi for millennia. The use of these medicines offered perspectives not otherwise seen or felt, and the medicines were respected as great teachers.

Today, scientific research increasingly supports the use of psilocybin in easing chronic depression and anxiety at end of life, particularly in cancer patients. Psilocybin is becoming more widely available medically, as are other psychedelics, and an increasing number of people are partaking and benefiting. In these instances, each individual's experience should be supported with education and preparation, correct dosage, a statement of intention, and careful supervision. The Multidisciplinary Association for Psychedelic Studies (MAPS) is a credible resource for information.

Institutions such as Johns Hopkins University and NYU are also researching the use of psychedelics in medicine, and Naropa University in Colorado offers a Psychedelic-Assisted Therapies Certificate. As exciting as it is that these therapeutic modalities are becoming more widely accepted, I think it's important to remember and honor the fact that ancient cultures and indigenous peoples have been using psychedelic medicines since long before recorded history. Like the work of the death doula is not new, neither is this form of medicine.

I have supported dying individuals through safely coordinated sessions and have witnessed psilocybin's benefits, such as a spiritual connectivity and calmness that otherwise might not have been possible. (Though, closer to active death, it's hard to know what kind of magic uncommunicative dying individuals are experiencing in their own natural processes.) One woman I worked with who was chronically depressed slowly weaned herself from her depression medication and then with her doctor's approval partook in a psilocybin session with me as her doula. For three full weeks following the session she had no need of her antidepressants and began enjoying her life once again. When the daily grind with terminal illness feels emotionally debilitating, a three-week vacation from despair is a great consolation. I have also witnessed the benefits of microdosing—one can find great solace in small medicinal doses and does not necessarily need to have a full "journey" experience.

Though psychedelics may not feel like a comfortable way to treat depression and anxiety in each person (because of a great variety of reasons), technology now offers an alternative that simulates a gentle psychedelic experience. I have had the unique experience of being an advisor and session facilitator for a virtual reality start-up whose focus is to reduce anxiety and existential dread through the journey of terminal diagnosis and to connect loved ones to each other though they may be far distances from each other physically. Though the experience is not as transcendent as an actual psychedelic experience has the potential to be, because the virtual reality environment is unlike everyday surroundings, and participants in the experience appear as a "cloud body" rather than a physical human form, the healing possibilities are boundless. It becomes so clear how much our physical appearance, facial expressions, and body language in everyday life impede our ability to truly, deeply listen to each other. In the therapeutic virtual reality environment, I have witnessed profound connectivity between humans at a time when expressing feelings can be an obstacle because of physical or emotional boundaries. In this calming and safe space, individuals and groups come together in a meaningful way that heals and changes lives.

At this time, it may not be possible to obtain therapeutic psychedelics or engage in a virtual reality session for the one dying, but an inquiry could still be made with the primary care physician.

LISTENING

At times, all a person needs is someone to listen. Fortunately, you do not need to be a therapist, doctor, or problem-solver to be a good listener.

The kind of listening needed is extremely intimate. It is spacious, nonjudgmental, and full of loving curiosity. We listen without judging what is being said and without an opinion that we want to impose. Listen to the dying person's words, watch their eye movements, notice what they do with their hands, and look with your heart at what is being said. It may feel heavy. Even if what they say doesn't seem important, every word and sound that is uttered *is* important, for their vocal cords will not be vibrating much longer. The last sounds will echo out into the universe, and we will replay them in our memory. Lean into that and truly listen.

- You may want to record what your loved one says. (Get permission whenever possible, and bear in mind that it may not be appropriate at times.) There may be messages for loved ones that come out in a jumbled mess of misordered words that make perfect sense to the one for whom the message was intended.
- Is there someone or something missing that would offer the dying person comfort? By actively listening, you may be able to pinpoint things they didn't even know they wanted or needed.
- Would the one who is dying like you to write letters or short notes for them, to be given to others after their death? Are there certain experiences they wish to share aloud before

they die? Ask them to tell stories they want remembered (and record, if they wish). What are the loose ends they would like help wrapping up?

❧ Of course, play music. There is always music. Perhaps the steady beat of a drum or the chords of a harp. I often use music or the analogy of floating away on a note to help guide those whom I work with out of their body. After words cease and there is only hearing, I think of this beautiful quote attributed to the eleventh-century Benedictine abbess Hildegard von Bingen: "When the words come, they are merely empty shells without the music. They live as they are sung, for the words are the body and the music the spirit."

ANCESTOR COMFORTS

Studying my own ancestry revealed an unseen world of connection. I feel like a more whole human with a mycelium-like web of blood relations surrounding me, despite time and distance. I feel like a wiser and more ancient being after learning about the land where my own flesh and blood walked. I researched the history of northwest Ireland and the southeast of Finland to find out which sicknesses, wars, famines, and turmoil had plagued people there, and I was able to guess at why my ancestors ventured to North America. From searching death records, I could see illnesses that swept through households and the deaths of many babies and children, particularly during Gorta Mór, the Great Famine (and oppression) that swept through Ireland from 1845–1852.

Before studying the paths of my ancestors, I had simply been intrigued by Ireland—I loved castles, harps, and fae folk! When

I traveled to Ireland to seek my ancestral lands, I had an entire itinerary planned that included the studying of banshees, sacred wells, and haunted castles. But something very different happened when I arrived. I got off the plane and sobbed. My knees felt weak and I could hardly get myself through customs. I felt the pain of the land and the people so deeply. And at the same time, I felt an overwhelming joy that I had returned home. I never ended up opening that planned itinerary.

With the assistance of a wonderful Irish woman named May, and a helpful gentleman in the town that I suspected my ancestors were from, I found the exact land of my family. The property, which dated back to at least the early 1800s, had long since been abandoned, but I was able to walk in through the open door. The floor was covered in two inches of sheep poop, and the walls were covered in moss. I looked into the intact hearth where food had been prepared, and I stood in the bedroom where babies were born and the sick and old died. My relatives were here, my family whose stories I am still uncovering after months of searching microfilm, old maps, emigration/immigration passenger lists, and church and census records. My mother's bloodline holds memories of cholera epidemics, fostered children, changed names, workhouses, and asylums, and we will likely never know the full stories of these lives. My family, and so many others in Ireland, held living wakes on the docks or at Droichead na nDeor, the Bridge of Tears, knowing that they would likely never see their families again after they left seeking a better life in America.

This is the land and these are the stories of the hauntings, the abandoned houses, and the wailing women whose pain and sorrow was tilled into the same fields that nourished their bodies. I didn't need to map out a trip of "haunted Ireland." I needed only to breathe the air and touch the stones to see, hear, and feel ghosts everywhere. These are my family's banshees, and it's clear that cellular memory and epigenetics play a role in my life, with odd and irrational fears. I am better in this present day for knowing the pains of my past.

I was fortunate to have family members who could share small bits of information about where they thought my great-grandparents were from. I realize this is not the case for everyone. Those who are adopted, who never knew one or both of their parents, or whose ancestors were enslaved may have difficulty in obtaining such details. Other obstacles such as burned or lost records may prevent you from finding ancestors.

Now readily available, DNA tests may provide you with a storyline and indicate your ancestors' place of origin. How wonderful to know that you were never and are never alone. Your ancestors had stories, you have a story—and that story matters. There is also nothing wrong with imagining a comforting ancestor for yourself. Take time to imagine the qualities that individual would have and welcome your ancestor to accompany you and watch over you while you walk your days on earth.

For both the one dying and the family members, taking time to pay homage to ancestors can feel like a bit of balm for the heart. Distance of time allows space in the sorrow and can help to normalize what's happening. It can serve as a reminder, even an acknowledgment and bonding between the one who lies in the bed and the one who stands alongside, that from the spiritual perspective there is no contrast of healthy and weak in the great cycle of life.

It's important to feel this connection on your deathbed—that your existence on earth matters, as did the existence of those who were alive and died before you. As the veil thins between living and death, many people have visions of their deceased loved ones. This is a common occurrence and is noted frequently by those who care for the dying.

It is not necessary to set foot upon your ancestral homeland, nor is it always appropriate or easy to do DNA testing. Connect with ancestors by listening to traditional music from your ancestral homeland, hold an item that once belonged to your oldest relative, look at a map, photos, or art and imagine a time when your ancestors lived there. If your ancestors lived on the very land that you reside on, listen to the tales the trees have to tell. Most trees live far longer than the average human, some easily dating back hundreds of years. Oh, what they have witnessed! The mycelium beneath our feet can stretch thousands of miles and live for thousands of years. During the dying process the mundane human perception of time and space holds little weight. For the dying, time and space are so closely interwoven with spirit that connectivity across great distances and between species is easily possible. Simply a desire and an imaginative thought of ancestral connection can be enough to request support and love from all directions.

TYING TOGETHER A TIMELINE

An understanding of earthly sequential time is something that begins to slip as dying approaches. Of course, timelines can also be a challenge for active caregivers who have entered into a timeless space where meals might be eaten at odd times or accidentally skipped. Yet, retaining some awareness of sequential events can be grounding and helpful at times when important mundane decisions need to be made. Sometimes we must transcend earthly time to piece together a timeline; this can be done in a trance or waking dream state. I call this work timeline retrieval. In essence, it is a spiritual life review.

A couple of times I have done timeline retrievals for the dying. Although this is not typical work for every modern death doula, I also do the work of ancient death doulas, who heal on multiple levels—not just the physical. I am quite comfortable with this work and have been time and space traveling since my earliest memories.

A gentleman I worked with was confused by his various procedures and could not retain enough information to make sound decisions. He continued to claim he wanted "everything to be done," even though he was quite close to death and had been informed that there was no hope of recovery.

The doctor, the palliative care team, and the man's son planned to meet the next morning to have a conversation with him. However, without having any recollection of the months of ER visits, chemotherapy, radiation, dehydration, double pneumonia, total confusion, and disorientation from space, time, and place, he didn't fully grasp the reasons why he was being advised to decline the "full code" (meaning *all* measures would be taken to save and revive him if he died). Those of us who were assisting him were frustrated, sympathetic, and confused ourselves.

That night, in a waking dream state, I brought him into my consciousness and he willingly arrived and stayed. (This is not and was not always the case.) I had only broad strokes of his life since childhood, but I had enough to start pulling the string of each event closer. One after the other, I pulled strings to bring the major events in his life closer, up to the current day (and I pulled that string closer as well). I did this with every milestone, every major trauma, every move across the world, and I tied them to his consciousness. Staying in this state is extremely difficult (for me, at least). However, with such an important meeting in the morning, I kept at it for hours—his life and death depended on it.

In the morning, his son reported after the meeting that the man had been clearer than he had seen him in months. The father recalled events and asked questions—to the surprise and delight of those present. He fully understood what was being asked of him. He understood that there was almost no chance of survival at this point. And when asked if he still wanted every-thing possible to be done, he said yes. That made me smile. His answer was clear. My job was done.

Creating a visual timeline with an individual can also be a helpful activity. This can be done with the one dying or with those who have known the person for an extended length of time. Some hours spent with the dying are more clear and event-focused, while others are in an alternate universe. It can be helpful during your loved one's wakeful times to show them where they are in their life's course, if you are able. Sometimes the elderly are shocked at how old they are. It's common for them to ask, "How old am I?" When you tell them, whether it has been one day or five minutes since they last asked, they can look at you like, "How did *that* happen? Are you sure?"

Above all, do not make the one dying (or anyone experiencing memory impairment) guess at your name or at the purpose of an event, and do not try to pry information from them. If recalling the past is uncomfortable, stick with the present.

SLEEP, REST, AND SEPARATION

People who are dying usually sleep for long periods of time (and this is good). Sleep and sleeplike states are needed as a person eventually transitions out of life. Creating an environment that supports sleep is a major goal in caring for the dying.

Scent, sound, and touch can all be extremely helpful in creating restful sleep. Sometimes just being left alone can also be beneficial to the person. If your loved one is unable to communicate clearly, it's up to you to choose what seems best.

✹ Herbal Support

There are many herbal sleep aids that are gentle and safe at end of life. Cannabis (which contains THC) is helpful, as is CBD (which contains very little THC). Lemon balm, chamomile, and valerian root can all make lovely bedtime teas. Also, essential oils of hops and lavender can be wonderful scented sleep aids. An herbal spray can be misted onto the pillow or drops added directly to the sheets. Dry aromatic herbs can be put in a sachet in or near the bed. Though not an herbal support, melatonin (naturally derived or synthetic) can be quite helpful in some circumstances, so check with the doctor.

TIME, SPACE, AND RHYTHM

Circadian rhythms do not exist for the dying. Day and night, time and space merge and separate as the human consciousness plays with transitioning out of the body. The one dying may even be more active at night and really challenge your boundaries as a caregiver.

When I worked night shifts by myself in a residential care home, I was often kept on my toes. Residents would be up and down, sometimes engaging in dreamlike activity around their rooms. Some who could not walk during the day suddenly had the ability to shuffle around the room with no assistance! It was my job to check on each resident every two hours. When I peeked in on them, I would have to determine whether their behavior was harmless enough or if I should try to put them back to bed. The phase of the moon often impacted the residents. The full moon, yes, but I found just as much (and even stranger) activity during the new moon phase.

Do not be alarmed if your loved one is suddenly able to talk and recalls a distant memory, then slips away again into deep sleep. The dying may call for or see ones who have died before them. They may report feeling light or heavy or at peace.

This can also be a time of unknowing. Your loved one may not know themselves as an individual and may not know you—even if you are their closest companion. This can be painful to witness. Try not to take it to heart. Tell them your name; tell them you are here to help. Seek another shoulder to cry on to help you through that pain.

SPIRITUAL SUPPORT

I have had the honor of sitting with corpses in my Buddhist community. We physically care for our own deceased and sit with them for three days straight, around the clock. There's a small team who cares for the corpse immediately after death, but it takes a village—or sangha, in this case—to continue to sit in attendance. This is not strange—it's what we believe is helpful for guiding the essence of the being through the bardo. (The bardo is a state between existence and nonexistence after the body has died and the remaining essence of "you" is undergoing a process of transition.)

During this time sitting with the body, it is impossible not to think of your own death. Later in the evening and through the night, it's just you (alive) and a corpse (dead) in a room. There have been some winter shifts where I felt so cold in the room that I wondered if the cooling implements (applied to the corpse to slow decomposition) needed to be maintained at all. The corpse did not seem to care one way or another.

I grew up in an Irish and Finnish Catholic family with open-casket wakes, and with parents who did not shelter me from seeing a dead body. I remember the day my grandfather died when I was twelve years old. My mother brought me with her to the nursing home to say goodbye to him. It was strange to see him not moving, and he looked as if he had been carved from wax. The overhead lights were on, which didn't help in creating any kind of sentimental mood (further causing the moment to seem somewhere between surreal and *very* real). That body was only a form; my grandfather was gone.

I imagined that the life force within him had kind of *evaporated* at the time. My mother asked me if I would like to kiss his forehead and I did. This, too, was bizarre because his skin was cold—not like from being outside on a winter day; my lips could find no warmth beneath the surface. Though these sensations and thoughts were foreign, they were not scary. My mother's tears were also foreign and painful, but not scary. After regularly talking to people about death and dying, I have learned that this kind of simple intimacy with a corpse—especially in childhood—is not always common.

I've sat with individuals who were religious their whole life but then decided near the end that God did not exist—or if "he" did, how cruel he must be to keep them alive when all their loved ones had died years ago. Then there is the exact opposite: people who were atheist their whole life but felt sure at the last minute that they were going to God.

It seems to me that religion and spirituality certainly play a role during times of death, but not necessarily more so than general ideas and interactions with death throughout life. What can make a real difference is the extent to which one can self-comfort and love, trust, and forgive oneself and others. We can try to understand the religious or spiritual life the person has lived, but their view might change a dozen times before their death, and they might never talk about it.

I grew up Catholic, in conjunction with my parents' newly affirmed New Age beliefs. I know the traditional prayers—and yet, when I told my parents that I could not only see faeries but that I also played with them, and that I was astral projecting, they confirmed what I was seeing and doing. Therefore,

I grew up with an all-loving, magical God, an acknowledgment of the sacred in everything, the possibility—even likelihood—of multidimensional worlds, and the notion of time as anything but linear. As a young teenager, I fell in love with the herbal witch world and lived in a Hindu ashram and later a Buddhist center—but I also hold value in my ancestors' practices of Celtic paganism and Sámi animism. I do not cling to or actively practice any one religion, but I find a great deal of comfort in Buddhist philosophies while living on earth.

This may sound strange to some readers, but this kind of broad spirituality is becoming more common among those who do not wish to claim a religion as well as those whose previous notions of religion no longer fit their expanding view of the world.

At times, prayers and texts from one's childhood can be deeply ingrained and bring comfort at the time of death, even if the individual has not been religious as an adult. In times of hardship families may have read from a religious text to bring some routine and a sense of being held by something larger and wiser. The dying time could be considered a hardship and therefore some of those same texts or prayers may feel comforting. It is always wise to ask in advance and never assume that the person wishes to engage in passages or prayers they may have turned to in the past—even the recent past.

In my opinion, there is one thing that transcends the myriad of religious and spiritual barriers: silent connection. Hold the dying person's hand, ever-so-gently stroke the top of their head, or sit close by holding space in great love.

REIKI FOR THE DYING

The chakra system is something we think of balancing while we are living, but it continues to play a role during the dying process as well. If you are a Reiki practitioner, and the person who is dying has given you permission to offer this to them during their transition, it can be a beautiful experience.

This is a process you can take part in whether or not you are touching the body, as each of the chakras vibrates, pulses, flares, and eventually ebbs. In fact, unless this is work you have previously done with the person, you should only offer Reiki support not just with hands hovering but from a distance such as outside of the room.

Long-distance Reiki is introduced in the second level of Reiki training; it allows practitioners to offer healing light from a distance, even from the other side of the planet. In the third or Master level, one is trained to offer Reiki through time and space. This can be a wonderful opportunity to offer healing to the younger or traumatized self of the one you are caring for. Emotional wounds that may have remained hidden for a very long time might surface as the individual undergoes a life review. Healing can happen on so many levels during the dying process.

Those who are untrained in Reiki should not be afraid to offer judgment-free, nonattached-outcome healing light to their loved ones. An established courtesy, however, is to get permission for healing from the one who you are offering it to. If this is not something you feel comfortable offering to your loved one, there are many trained practitioners who offer this service. An internet search will yield results—remember that they do not necessarily need to be in physical attendance to offer this healing. Hospitals and care facilities sometimes have staff or volunteers that are trained in Reiki as well.

I hold a Master Teacher level in Reiki and have offered Reiki and Phowa (a Vajrayana Buddhist method of transferring consciousness at the time of death) to several dying individuals in person and from a distance. Sometimes it is accepted freely as a cosmic gift. Other times, the rejection is perfectly clear. Each situation and each individual is different. I am thankful that I grew up with a mother who is an energy worker and Reiki Master Teacher who taught me about boundaries and these sensitivities from a very early age. Be sensitive enough to recognize when the person dying communicates their wishes nonverbally, and don't hold on to a particular desired outcome.

I used both Reiki and Phowa with my father-in-law in the ICU when he was being extubated and taken off life support. His daughter and son sat on one side of him, holding his hand. On the other side, I held one of my hands on his heart chakra and the other on the top of his head. While the physical heart remained beating for some time and was holding strong, his crown chakra became an upward rushing waterfall of energy. It was so powerful and so immense that I kept looking to see if anything could be seen. But, no. This was the essence of life force, unable to be seen with the meager human eye.

A TIME FOR SHRINES

Setting up a shrine can be a wonderful way to celebrate the preciousness of an individual's life. Candles, photos, flowers, special rocks, and items the person loves are all appropriate to add to the shrine. Favorite drinks or foods are also lovely things to add.

Often it is appropriate to add photos of deceased friends and family members or ancestors of the one who is dying. This shows that they are not forgotten. Their lives impacted the world; their lives mattered. This can be a comfort to the one who is dying— a reminder that they too will be remembered and honored, and that there are others who have died before them.

A shrine can be established anywhere in the room, around the house, or outside, and you can invite people to add to it when they visit. This gives close friends and relatives an opportunity to care for the shrine, arrange it on a daily basis, and continue to tend to it even after the person has died. A shrine placed in the room of the one dying also gives people something to "do" or look at if they are uncomfortable visiting.

Children may wish to set up their own shrine for the one who is dying, either in the room itself or in their own space. Meaningful objects linked to the one dying can include items such as a stuffed animal they played with together or favorite books they read together. It can be helpful to put something on the shrine for the child to tend to when they visit, such as a small plant that is visibly growing, a puzzle that can be added to, or small objects (such as pebbles or wildflowers) that they've collected from nature. These will signify that time is passing and that things continue to grow, change, expand, and also die.

Alternative Location

Even in an ICU, a small, portable shrine is possible. LED candles can be used instead of real ones and a dish or pouch of dried lavender can be just as lovely as a bouquet of flowers.

Six

Discomforts during Caregiving

Life can only be understood backwards; but it must be lived forwards.

SØREN KIERKEGAARD

*I*n highly charged emotional situations, it can be challenging to know what do to and what to think. In a room full of people centered around caring for the one dying, feelings and opinions can overlap, creating further confusion, which can feel thick and sticky. In this chapter we'll take a look at some of the discomforts that can arise and some ways of inviting a sense of emotional space.

EXPRESSING THE VERY DIFFICULT

There are times when something really needs to be said that could be upsetting to the one who is dying. Alternately, the person dying can say things that can be upsetting to those who are

104

caregiving or visiting. If you witness this interaction, know that every two people have their very own relationship—even their own karma, if you will. We cannot fully understand the relationship between two people, therefore it is impossible to perceive what is healing and what is painful.

As a general rule, however, it is most valuable to say whatever needs to be said with the intention of healing. Perhaps one must say to a dying father, "You abused me my entire childhood and I am still so sad and in so much pain from that." That is different than saying, "You ruined my life." The same painful stories can come forth and air out, the difference is in the delivery and the intention. Words matter. Intention matters. If you or others must say unpleasant things to someone who is dying, think of how you might wish to hear the words on your own deathbed. You are the one who will go on living, and the words you say and the way you choose to express your feelings may linger with you long after your loved one's death.

Similarly, we hope the same goes for the person dying—that they won't say anything unless it is with the intention of healing. This is not always the case, unfortunately. People often say painful things from their deathbed, and we, the living, must carry these words with us. Sometimes secrets are revealed by the dying, sending the family into emotional chaos. Sometimes painful hallucinations will be expressed, and sometimes the dying need to share information that has been weighing on them their whole life. Sometimes we will not know what is true and what is not.

Through pain and confusion and elation, try not to tell yourself too many stories—remain curious as much as possible.

WORDS ARE NOT ALWAYS
WHAT IS NEEDED

While working at a nursing facility I overheard two gentle-
men talking one morning. One was significantly older than
the other, and the younger man admired his friend for being a
World War II veteran. The younger gentleman explained how
he wished he could have served in the war, but he had been too
young. He then said to the other, "You're ninety-five. That's a
real good age to get to." The older man very gently said, "I've
lost my wife, my children, my siblings, my parents, my aunts
and uncles, and all of my cousins. I'm the only one left." The
younger man just listened and bowed his head. He didn't offer
pity or try to console him, nor did he seem to feel bad that his
own feelings were not considered in that comment. The older
man meant nothing more than what he said, and the younger
man interpreted it exactly as it was meant. They just sat side
by side. Gently.

WHEN WHAT IS HAPPENING IS
AGAINST YOUR DESIRES

It is not uncommon for the person who is dying to make decisions that others do not agree with. Sometimes the person does
not want to pursue medical treatment—even when the progno-
sis seems quite good. If this decision is made early on, it may
be upsetting to others throughout the active dying process. It's
helpful to remember that these kinds of choices are extremely
individual.

There are times when the dying person begins a rapid decline, has second thoughts, and wants to begin treatment. Or loved ones may begin to panic and beg the dying person to start treatment. Unfortunately, this is a common scenario and painful for everyone involved, since it may be too late.

All too often, a partial or total denial of dying is present. This can be upsetting to loved ones and caregivers who want to create meaningful time, but the one dying will not engage.

In these instances, breathing and self-care practices can be helpful. Beginning any kind of new practice amid emotional upheaval can be challenging, but you need to just begin where you are.

You, the caregiver, may wish to express your thoughts and feelings to the one who is dying, or you may wish to talk to another individual who is slightly removed from the situation.

If you choose to speak to someone outside your inner circle, try to find someone who has been in a similar situation and is more likely to understand what you're experiencing. Look for someone who will mostly listen instead of giving advice or sharing opinions.

If you choose to express your thoughts to the one who is dying, remember that you, too, will have your own experience and choices in dying one day (if you are lucky). At this time, you view life from a different perspective than the one who is dying. You can guess what your loved one is feeling, but you cannot know.

Rather than simply sharing your opinions, thoughts, and feelings with the person dying, try to remain curious and ask questions. Look for routes and paths that have been forged in this person's life, and try to discover if their decision seems consistent with their lifestyle. You may find that while you do not like their choice or viewpoint, it is consistent with how they have lived their life.

At times, you may encounter the exact opposite. One who has lived a fully organic and holistic life may decide to try all the medical interventions possible to further their life. This, too, is their choice to make.

WHAT TO DO WHEN THERE IS NOTHING TO DO

There are times when there is no place for the main caregiver or death doula. No place for being helpful—physically, emotionally, or otherwise. Yet you're there, perhaps feeling like you *want* to engage.

First, know that there are times when the situation has nothing to do with you—and, therefore, you should have the ability to step back with grace. This can be difficult, especially if you can see exactly what is needed but your offer to help is blocked in one way or another.

My mother and I like to practice a version of the Catholic novena (nine days or weeks of consecutive prayers, typically with a rosary) called Mary, Undoer of Knots. In this practice, you envision the untangling of knots and call upon Mother Mary to assist you. In this instance, the knots would be your own tangled feelings about how you think an event surrounding death should unfold.

⚜

MINDFULNESS PRACTICE
Tonglen Meditative Breathing

You may wish to practice a Tibetan Buddhist breathing technique of giving and taking (also called sending and taking)
called *tonglen*. You can practice this on your own, ideally taking
time to learn it when you are in a safe, non-charged environment (rather than on the spot in a tense situation).

*Begin by activating a feeling of loving-kindness. Often this kind
of feeling can be sparked by imagining something that you have
no negative affiliation with, such as a pile of puppies playing
gently. Take a moment to think of something, and make note
of the feeling that arises in you. Invite that feeling to grow and
permeate your being—filling you with a sense of loving-kindness.*

*Next, in your imagination, place in front of you the one
whose pain you desire to have lifted from them. As you inhale,
imagine drawing in the pain from the other person (or situation)
where it is naturally transformed within the space of loving-
kindness that you have prepared within you. As you exhale,
imagine filling the person with that same love.*

*With this kind of meditative breathing, you are transforming the
pain or agitation into purified love, calm, peace, or whatever remedy
is needed. This practice will not harm you. You are not absorbing
any of the pain yourself and it does not accumulate. It is simply
transforming in space—and your loving intention is doing the work.*

*When you get tired, simply stop the practice. Let it all go and
get a nice drink of water.*

⚜

As you can imagine, you must do this breathing activity from a place of total strength and calm, and you must understand that you are not depleting your own energy as you do this. When you do this in a painful situation or for a being that is in pain, you feel so strong that you say to yourself, "Let me take a bit of that from you, let me take some of your pain." And then when you exhale, you are thinking, "Take a bit of this peace, I can offer you relief." In this way you are continuing to offer more kind, gentle, neutral energy into the world.

If you're looking for additional thoughts on this practice, American Tibetan Buddhist nun and teacher Pema Chödrön explains the tradition beautifully in her book *Tonglen: The Path of Transformation.*

As a private duty nurse, I once sat overnight with a woman who was 104 years old and in an active phase of dying. Though she was dying simply of old age, her body was still very strong. She used no walker, no hearing aid, and pull-up underwear only at night "just in case." Around two o'clock in the morning, her breathing started to become laborious and constricted; she sat bolt upright at the end of her bed and started pulling at her nightgown. I asked if she would like some water or a back rub or if I could sing her a song. She didn't answer. In fact, she was not really in this world. She pulled off her nightgown, then wanted it back on. She wanted socks on and socks off, nightgown on and off. She was not panicking, just obsessive. She had no meds that could be given, so I just sat with her. I was there if she needed any assistance and made sure she did not hurt herself, but mostly I was there to simply breathe and witness. Since there was nothing I could *do* for her that evening, I did the one thing that felt helpful: I released the way I thought it should go, engaged the tonglen breathing technique, and sat with her in loving space until she fell asleep.

LANGUAGE BARRIERS IN THE DYING PROCESS

Those who are nearing death often partially or fully return to their native tongue, no matter how long they've spoken another language. My father-in-law began returning to his first language (Spanish) as his terminal illness progressed. We were fortunate to find a fully bilingual Latina pulmonary specialist in Vermont, though we didn't find her until his last four days. It would have been easier, linguistically, for my father-in-law to pass away in his home country of Chile, but he would not have had all the family care he received by living close to and with us. My husband and I and my sister-in-law were his primary caregivers, and I was also a confidante of his. During his last few months, I found myself feeling ashamed that I could not speak Spanish at a time when he needed language support so desperately. His son and daughter translated when they were present, but otherwise we had to make a constant effort to be sure the nurses were using a translation app to communicate with him. This was difficult when he was in and out of so many hospitals. Though it lacked intimacy, technology played a crucial role in these vulnerable circumstances, so for this we were thankful.

Not every death goes as everyone wishes, so we all make adjustments. My father-in-law had been traveling freely as a single man for the last three years of his life and had not established a true home base. Without knowing his death was imminent, and because of a variety of hardships and decisions, his death nesting was done as a free spirit between multiple countries. It was a beautiful end-of-life journey but made actively dying difficult.

If you have the ability to speak two or more languages, please consider volunteering your time visiting with and advocating for those who are isolated in this way while dying.

. . . .

Worrying About Not Worrying

During an overnight shift as acting nurse (as an LNA) in a residential facility, I was paged by a resident at 3:00 a.m. I swallowed a big swig of my yerba mate and hurried to her room to help her to the bathroom. She paged me every night around this time so that I could assist her to the toilet, even though she had already gone in her pull-up. The bathroom trip meant we could chat for a moment. She initiated this, as I usually remained quiet unless invited to engage. Likely, she used to chat with her husband in the middle of the night long ago. Though she had lost most of her memory, the routine trip to the bathroom and the midnight chat remained.

As I tucked her back into bed she said, "You know, I'm really worried about something." I replied, "Yes? What's the problem?" I imagined she was concerned about her children or an upcoming doctor appointment. She said, "I'm worried that I have nothing to be worried about." Her answer surprised me. I realized that to many people, worry can feel productive. Since she had no real idea what was going on beyond that very moment, and everything seemed fine, she felt like she was missing something.

How does one console someone who is worried about nothing? I did what I would do with my child who is afraid of monsters: I tucked her into bed, held her hand, and reminded her that she was fed and clothed, warm and safe, and that soon the morning birds would awaken. I knew that she would soon drift off and sleep through the first bird song (and need to be awakened for breakfast), but these simple reminders of presence were enough to help her go back asleep.

. . . .

MEDICAL AID IN DYING

Medical aid in dying is a form of hastening death that is an option in some states and countries. *MAiD,* as it is currently referred to in the United States and Canada, can be as controversial as abortion. As a death doula I neither approve of nor condemn this form of hastening death. Rather, I care for the one dying in the manner they and their family have chosen.

No death is easy, no death is without consequences—and medical aid in dying is no different. There can still be pain, confusion, anger, and fear. Resentment and regrets can still bubble up—not just for the one dying but for all who surround them. Each individual experiences a death differently (even people together in a room, witnessing the same scene). This applies to medically assisted death as well.

Making decisions during sensitive times can seem nearly

impossible. Sometimes we take so long to make a decision that the options change, and previous options are no longer available. Sometimes, having the option to end your life on your own timeline in a location of your choice feels like a bit of control (when so many other things feel out of your control). In the United States, some people who get the prescription never ingest the medication. In other countries, a doctor is the only one who can administer the injection.

Like euthanasia for animals, medical aid in dying is a privilege not everyone on our planet is able to access. Many people die without pain medication, let alone a doctor's prescription for ending life on one's own timeline. If you or a loved one is interested in this option, you can speak to your doctor. Not every doctor will feel comfortable prescribing the medication, even if the patient is receiving hospice care and has a life expectancy of six months or less.

Those who have had poor or no medical care, people of color who have been grossly mistreated by the healthcare system, and those who have physical disabilities may have a great mistrust of medical aid in dying. It's important to remain sensitive: what might seem like a right to some is considered dangerous or even insulting to others.

. . . .

MAiD and Death Doulas: Tête-à-tête

I will not disapprove of your medically assisted death. I will not tell you not to seek it. I will not tell you to let your body die a "natural death." I will not tell you to hold out for a miracle or a cure or more time.

I will not approve of your medically assisted death. I will not tell you you're doing the right thing. I will not say that your reasons are justified. I will not tell you this is the right way to hasten death if you are terminally ill, nor tell you that this is the way out of your pain.

If you ask to know more about MAiD, I will provide you with as much information as I have at that time. This information will consist of laws, timing, and concoctions or injections. I cannot tell you what it feels like to ingest or receive the medication. I cannot tell you how your family and friends and community will react to your death—whatever manner of death is chosen. I cannot tell you what it is like to die.

I do not condone, I do not condemn, I do not judge. I do not make the laws, I do not advocate for the laws, I do not protest the laws.

I am watching. I am listening. I am feeling from one body away from yours, trying to anticipate your needs.

I will pen your goodbye letters. I will draw the curtains or open the door. I will rub your temples; I will massage your feet. I will pray with you, help you find "the key," and be awestruck as you say to me, "My mother is here." I will sit alongside you for your last breath and remain still through the time your breath does not return, when, instead, I will focus on my own breath.

I serve so that you can feel loved, safe, and witnessed in your state of, and exit from, Being. *This* is a doula-assisted death.

. . . .

COMING UPON AN ACCIDENT
OR SUDDEN DEATH

One evening during a shift at a residential care facility, I reported to the nurse on duty that one of the residents was walking strangely. The nurse said, "Yes, he always walks a little strange." However, since I was the one who gave this gentleman his biweekly showers and monitored his physical movements, I knew better. I returned to check on him and rounded the corner just as he collapsed, unconscious and retching vomit. The nurse had heard the fall and came running as I dropped to the floor to attend to him. I checked his pulse and carefully watched his breathing as I spoke calmly to him: "John, you have collapsed. Your body is having a hard time. You fell to the floor. Help is coming. Your family is coming. You are in good hands and you are not alone." I rolled him onto his side, stroked his head, rubbed his back, and cleaned the vomit from his mouth as he went in and out of consciousness. I repeated his name and spoke clearly about what was going on, assuring him he'd be taken care of until the ambulance arrived. I was able to do all of this because the nurse was calling the ambulance. For those fifteen minutes, my only job in the world was to care for and love that man as if he were my child. He died in the hospital not long after that.

Emergencies do happen, even when one is at home on hospice and there is a foreseeable, "expected" death. An unexpected death, or the need to get emergency help, can arise and require a different kind of care than the slow, intimate care you may have been providing. Since the bathroom is the most common place for injuries to occur, because there are so many hard and slippery surfaces, it's wise to take extra precautions when making trips to the restroom. It's important to know that although a do-not-resuscitate order means that you do not try to bring the person back to life after they have died, it does not mean that you do not attempt to save them if they are injured.

I have always stopped at roadside accidents to see if help is needed. Sometimes there is plenty of aid and I would only be in the way, so I retreat. Other times, it seems people assume everything is being taken care of when it's not.

If you feel capable, you can offer support when coming across an accident, no matter where it is. Perhaps it is only to call 911 or to warn oncoming traffic, but the work of a death doula is not confined to slow, coordinated deaths. We can swoop in and fade out as needed. The key is to know what role is called for in that moment. There are times when a death doula's role is to remain invisible and only witness, hold space, or breathe. If it is safe for you to engage and you feel called to physically help, then your role might be much more hands-on. Remember to scan the scene for possible dangers, use your hazard lights, and don't be afraid to give spectators jobs to do while you tend to the accident victims. People are often willing to call 911, even if they do not feel safe exiting their vehicle. We do not want to cause accidental harm to ourselves or others.

If emergency death doula work feels like something you might do, learn about universal precautions and consider completing basic first aid training. As always, remember to step back when the rescue team arrives. I would love to see the role of doula incorporated into emergency rescue teams.

Seven

Talking with Children about Death and Dying

He is gone, in the sky, and his body is in the earth . . .
But you still got him in your heart, and in your phone.
AMAIA LUNA, AGE 3
(CONSOLING HER FATHER ON THE
DEATH OF HIS FATHER)

*C*hildren often want to be helpers, and there are plenty of tasks they can assist with when their loved one is dying. It is almost always appropriate for them to sit nearby or on the bed and read a book quietly. That is how a child sits vigil.

Keep in mind that some situations in acute care can be alarming for children. At the same time, children are resilient and usually do as well with death as the adults around them do. Carefully weigh every situation.

It can be helpful to talk to children about death and dying when they are quite young, so that they have an idea of what to expect when someone they love is in the process of dying. If they have helped bury a dragonfly, mouse, or bird before (and it was not traumatic), they can begin to view death as natural, rather than traumatic and scary. When the seasons and the lives of plants are talked about in terms of death and the return of new life, this can help children understand the wholeness of the life cycle.

TINY DEATHS AND BIG DEATHS

In an ideal world, we would have plenty of time to talk to our children and other sensitive people before each death—to avoid painful surprises. While this isn't always possible, there are many ways we can acknowledge and discuss the cycle of life on a daily basis.

My cat delivers dead mice, birds, and squirrels to our doorstep regularly. Driving down the road, dragonflies hit the windshield, animals lie dead on the side of the road, and neighborhood pets die. These are what I like to call tiny deaths, and they happen around us all the time. Other deaths that play a role in life are found in nature with plants and trees. We can watch the flowers grow in spring, blossom in summer, wither in fall, and die in winter. We become fond of trees if we let ourselves, so when a favorite tree falls in a storm or gets chopped down, we can feel sadness.

If we talk about these tiny deaths with our children, it provides a framework, making big deaths feel more natural and less scary. Big deaths are things like the loss of our human companions, caregivers, siblings, or children. For many, the loss of a pet feels just as strong or even stronger than the loss of a parent. It is all very individual.

Treat tiny deaths with respect. Look at the body of the dead mouse. Notice it is not moving, it is not breathing. Ask the child how they think it died. Notice these daily deaths and talk about how the life and death of that little being mattered. Take a moment to have a ceremony, even if the ceremony is only to say, "I'm sorry," or "Return to the earth." This careful consideration for death in small beings will help when the bigger deaths arrive so that children have practiced what to say and how to acknowledge the death.

Children experiencing the death of a human or animal can sometimes display great wisdom, clarity, and calm. (This excludes close, tragic deaths.) If this happens, it is not necessarily because they do not understand. Remember that children are still new to life and before culture, society, and parenting teaches them otherwise, nothing is unnatural, out-of-order, or wrong—including death.

As difficult as it is, we must acknowledge that miscarriages, stillbirths, and the deaths of children and babies happen. These deaths are excruciating for the parents—never fully healed or forgotten. As a funeral celebrant, I encourage shrines and ceremonies to acknowledge the lives of these small, precious beings. One woman I know held a ceremony thirty years after giving birth to her stillborn child. The newborn had been taken away by the hospital staff and she was never allowed to hold him. It is never too late to ceremonially acknowledge an important event.

Over the years, I have found myself concerned not only about my own children's safety but their friends' safety as well. The death of a playmate is sad and confusing. The deaths of my own children's friends by suicide and accident have impacted and changed their lives from a young age. This is nothing that we can protect them from, but we do have the ability to listen carefully to their concerns and sorrows and let them know that their feelings are heard. Depending on their ages and the situation, they may want space or time with their friends or they may cling to you for support. Sometimes hosting a group of kids who can mourn together can be really beneficial no matter what their age. Make sure there is plenty of food and drink and perhaps invite activities that inspire sharing aloud in whatever way feels appropriate.

A CHILD'S TOOL KIT

Children, teens, and even adults may benefit from the various practices provided in this part of the book. These tools are offered to assist and support them during difficult emotional times and in discussions about death and dying.

Mists

It can be helpful to create a mist that can be applied to the body or sprayed in the air and used when visiting a sick, dying, or deceased loved one. Perhaps offer your child a couple of mists to choose from, based on how they are feeling at that particular visit. In some (supervised) cases it may be appropriate and enjoyable for a child to share a mist with a dying loved one.

To make your mists, simply fill a 2- or 4-ounce spray bottle with purified water and add just a few drops of your chosen essential oil.

- **Mist for Courage:** Geranium or peppermint
- **Mist for Calming:** Lavender, jasmine, or chamomile
- **Mist for Love:** Rose and vanilla or ylang-ylang
- **Mist for Remembrance:** Lilac, rosemary, or lily of the valley
- **Moon Water Mist:** Charge water under a full moon to make an unscented but powerful mist for clarity, courage, and love. A gemstone or special pebbles can be added for extra strength.
- **Sun Water Mist:** Charge water by the bright sun of day to make an unscented and powerful mist for soothing, wakefulness, and remembrance. A gemstone can be added for extra strength.

Amulets

People of all ages may appreciate an amulet that can be worn as a necklace or bracelet or kept close in a pocket. An amulet can be a single object or a whole little collection of things that make you feel strong.

For example, perhaps a coin that your grandpa gave you can turn into your lucky coin. Perhaps a special rock that your child finds and carries in a pocket can be a reminder to plant wiggly toes firmly on the earth.

You can make a small closeable amulet pouch by cutting out the pocket of an old pair of pants and tying it shut with ribbon. One example is an amulet pouch for courage: add a stone to remember the earth, a feather to remember gentleness, a pretty seed or shelled nut to remember the great mystery of life, and a scroll of birch bark with a favorite quote written on it.

Imaginative Play and Puppets

Children can use imaginative play while processing death. They may want to wear a stethoscope around their neck like the nurse or wear a crown of flowers to become a fairy healer or witch doctor. When a child is "working" with a real human, explain that the objective is not to heal the patient and return them to good health but rather to care for, love, and serve the one who is dying. When playing on their own with their teddy bears and dolls, they can imagine whatever they would like—including miraculous recoveries.

Puppet play can explain and reveal much. Try having a wise puppet speak plainly about death to another puppet who will listen carefully. Remember, the wise one does not need to be big and powerful—a small puppet could be tucked into a pocket, backpack, or purse in case some wisdom is needed on the go.

Have one puppet ask plain questions, such as, "Why is Grandpa dying?" The wise puppet can reply, "Every living being has a life cycle. It's very natural. Grandpa's life cycle is coming to an end, so he will die." You can also talk about age and death, perhaps beginning with the life cycle of a sea turtle, fox, or bat. Ask them, "What do you think the life span of a unicorn might be?"

It's okay to tell a child that you do not have all the answers to all their questions. You can look up some answers together, and let some remain a mystery. Assure them that they will always be cared for and loved.

Keys

The magic of a key can be understood by young and old alike. Keys unlock doors, keep things safe, and symbolize secrets, privacy, magical realms, alternate universes, and different realities. I have never met a child who does not love a special key, and I have never known an adult who does not have a key (or dozens) of their own.

Keys can be a powerful tool when discussing death. A key can open the door to an imaginary room where a conversation can be had with a loved one who has died. A key can close a sacred box for storing thoughts and feelings that can be examined and revisited. Sometimes a box from a childhood trauma is kept and can be opened and examined in a safe space as a teenager or adult.

Bubbles

Bubbles can carry messages to the one who has died. When a bubble pops, where does it go? Well, everywhere! Intentions or messages can be blown into a bubble so that when it pops, its contents merge with the atmosphere and space itself—a place without boundaries. This can also be an imaginative activity. In bed at night, a child (or an adult, for that matter) can send messages in imaginary bubbles to their loved one.

Bubbles can also be used to ease scary feelings. Since anything can be put inside a bubble, it can hold anger, hatred, or anxiety. Direct the child to pull the emotion out of their body and blow it into the bubble. Ask them, "Where in your body do you feel the anger?" If they say their belly, they can blow from that exact spot in their belly and fill the bubble. Send it out their bedroom window, into the sky, past the clouds, and deep into space—noting how it gets smaller and smaller as it gets farther away. Repeat as needed. You may find yourself trying this, too.

Colors, Forms, and Smells

Sometimes children are too little to name their feelings. Even as adults, we sometimes don't quite know what we are feeling—perhaps because we are overwhelmed or haven't let ourselves sit with an uncomfortable feeling long enough to get to know it. Ask the child (or yourself), "What color is your feeling? What is the texture of your feeling? What does it sound like? What does it smell like?" More often than not, even small children will be able to do this exercise pretty easily. Next we ask, "How can the feeling be eased? Can it melt? Can it explode? Can it shimmer away?" This might be a good time for a key or wand.

From Space to Ants

Another exercise can look at "big view" and "little view." If the child is having a hard time comprehending the entire situation, look for a magnifying glass or a compass. Try to bring the child's focus down and in. A compass can lead you somewhere, but not unless you carefully watch the directions close at hand. A magnifying glass naturally leads you to things that are small. What are the ants doing today? Has that seed sprouted? If the child's view is tight and fixated, try watching hot air balloons or boats leaving port—anything that starts close and leads away.

Just lying on your back and watching clouds with a child, looking for shapes, can help bring the focus farther away. Outer space is the ultimate unknown, and some kids (and adults) find great comfort in that!

Telephones

Telephones can help you talk about feelings or get messages to those who have died. There's a vintage rotary phone in my house, which I have picked up and made confessions into. Did anyone hear it? No, but I said it aloud—and not just to an empty room. I said it with intention, into a device that was created to transmit spoken messages. After my daughter's grandfather died, she wanted to text him. I let her draw a picture on my cell phone and send it. When I asked if she remembered he had died, she said, "Yes, but he would really like that drawing."

PET AND ANIMAL DEATHS

I grew up with a myriad of animals: horses, dogs, cats, chickens, pigs, turkeys, rabbits, hamsters, guinea pigs, and fish. We did not have cows but our neighbors grazed theirs in our field and I played in their barn down the road. On our road there were six houses, which held fifteen people, and probably two hundred animals within the same stretch of land (about two miles). I spent long hours sitting in my hayloft playing with the latest batch of kittens, traipsing through the forest with my dogs, and reading books to my horse in the stable. Some mama cats were so clever that they would give birth and nest with their babies in secret places that were really hard to find. I would search in every dark crawl space, between floor boards, and in the back of buildings we never used.

One cold winter I found a litter of kittens that the mama had abandoned in my father's toolshed. It was a litter of five and they all appeared to be completely frozen. This was so sad. We picked them up in a cardboard box and brought them inside to warm by the fire. One little one was the first to move and we fed her warm milk from a very tiny bottle. Two more slowly began moving. The last two were dead. Their little bodies thawed, but they had no life. The three miracle kittens mewed and flexed their claws and purred while we bottle fed them multiple times a day for the rest of the winter.

This was an incredible and educational Extreme Rescue Adventure of Life and Death in Northern Vermont. I could not believe I had to go to school each morning and leave the tiny kittens for the day—clearly *this* was so much more important than sitting in a classroom with a textbook. This experience made such an impression on me that even now, almost thirty-five years later, I remember it well. I can even recall the distinct smell of the kittens—who had been born in a box of old oily rags from the toolshed—and how eventually we washed that smell off.

Some of our animals died of natural causes (we just found them dead one day), some of them ran off into the forest or were eaten by coyotes, foxes, or bobcats, and some of them died so slowly that we had to make the decision whether or not to euthanize. (The pigs did not die a natural death. This is why I have now been a vegetarian for thirty-five years.)

When animals died of natural causes, we would usually look at the body, cry, and talk about what might have happened. Then my father would find a spot on the property to bury them. On the other hand, when the dying process of our dogs became too much for my mother to bear, we called the vet to come. Through copious tears, we bore witness as our family pet's life ended. After, we would say "sorry" and "thank you" and "I love you," and pet their fur. My father would find a lovely spot along the forest's edge to bury them.

As an adult with my own children, I have let our pets die natural deaths when they are not severely injured. My children held our guinea pigs until their last breaths, with tears streaming down their faces. Then we would decorate a special box and bury the animal in a special place. This was my children's first experience caring for a living being through the dying process. Being an animal death doula can be powerful for both children and adults.

Making decisions about hastening death is never easy. Since birth and death are simply what humans and animals experience on our planet, I encourage people to allow them to be as natural as they are, whenever possible. It can sometimes be easier for a child to talk about and experience death in animals before humans. If a parent is willing to let their child witness an animal laboring and giving birth (as parents often do, even if it's via a TV show and not in real life), I believe children should be allowed to witness an animal laboring through dying.

When a mother dog is giving birth, she pants, lies down, won't eat or drink, sometimes moans, and is not herself. This can go on for an extended period and can be worrisome. However, because the feeling is one of hope and elation, we let the mother dog labor with little or no intervention and will allow children to watch.

All the same stresses of labor exist for an animal who is laboring in dying. However, because we equate death with an absence of hope and only sorrow, we often do not want to watch, do not want children to watch, and commonly choose euthanasia for the animal if we can afford that. Around the world, and for those who cannot afford veterinary care, euthanasia is not always an option. Though we might still have the urge to end an animal's suffering, we may have to resort to other options to end the animal's pain. Backyard deaths are not uncommon, and many near-dead animals have met merciful humans along roadsides. There is room for death doula care then as well—holding calm love in your heart while you do what you feel needs to be done.

If you choose euthanasia for an animal and you have children, communicate carefully when explaining what is happening. It is not uncommon for a child to ask a question like, "Is Grandma going to be euthanized like Toto?"

I would encourage anyone who is willing to witness and serve as doula at the birth of an animal to consider witnessing and being a doula in their death as well.

When witnessing both birthing and deathing (especially with children or those who are extremely sensitive), it is important to take breaks, go for walks, and drink lots of water, since you'll be processing many emotions.

Death Doulas for Animals

I have been asked many times to be a death doula for an animal, and each time I have been there for the human. I remind people that they are their pet's best death doula and that having me show up during the active dying process may be more disruptive than helpful, as it could draw the animal out of its zone or secret nesting. You are the one who knows best how to love and serve your pet.

Over the course of my childhood my family had five horses, at least fifty cats, and almost a dozen dogs. When an animal was in pain, it was not uncommon for it to come to us for help. As an adult, I have treated urinary tract infections with small amounts of diluted cranberry juice and have performed minor surgeries on my cats, giving them natural antibiotics such as manuka honey to promote healing and prevent infection. If it's a concern I can treat for my children, it's usually something I can treat in my pets.

Remember, though, that when an animal is dying, its instinct may be to die on its own. Cows out to graze will not come back to the barn; if you let a dog out to pee, it might not want to come back in; a house cat will retreat to the furthest depths of a closet. Like some humans, animals will often wait to leave their body until you leave the room. When you can instinctively feel this, it can be very hard to give them space to let go.

I encourage people to actively take part in their animals' lives and make memories throughout their time together. Take photos at the beach and park, give them their favorite treats, make paw art with paint or clay, and learn how to give them massages. Do these memory-making activities when they feel great—so that when they are *not* feeling their best, you can allow them space to do what feels natural to them.

After they have died, you can lay out their body in the same manner you might lay out a human body. Comb their fur, place them on a bed of flowers, wrap them in their favorite blanket, tell them you love them, and share their death story with others. If your pet has died in a veterinary hospital and does not have a communicable disease, you may ask to take the body back with you for a home funeral. Note that you may need to place a pad beneath your pet while transporting and laying out the body, to absorb or catch any elimination.

I was once invited to an elaborate and beautiful animal funeral. A lovely tent was set up in a backyard overlooking the dog's favorite pond. Guests gathered around the shrine to share cookies and stories; poems were read and dragonflies—the ones that the dog liked to chase—danced over the pond. It was incredibly sentimental and, indeed, more meaningful than some human funerals I have attended. I assisted the woman by helping her create glass teardrop- and heart-shaped pendants with her dog's cremains.

It can be beautiful to honor your pet's life with a home funeral or memorial service, and it can be a great introduction to funerals for those who have never attended one for a human. Our pets are some of our biggest teachers.

Eight
After the Last Breath

*Grieving is a cleansing; a way to reclaim and recover
our spirit.*

SOBONFU SOMÉ

*A*n expected death is not an emergency for the hospice patient who dies at home or in the hospital. Though even in instances when the impending death is discussed and prepared for (or even scheduled, in cases of MAiD or a removal from life support), it can still feel jarring when it happens. When you have been caring for your ailing loved one for a while and they eventually breathe their last breath, there is sometimes the tendency to quickly go get someone, call someone, or do *something* when they die.

Instead, this is a good time to pause. Let the clocks stop. Place the hourglass on its side. In this vacancy, in this *no space in time,* there is a great heaviness, a great spaciousness, an immense emptiness, and a fullness that is incomparable. Feel into the space. A question of *What now?* may form in your mind, but you don't have to take the bait. Instead, in the moments after death, just s t o p. If you are able to let go of any kind of *knowing,* you may find that you can feel the largeness of the human spirit. Rest in that awe.

The moments and days (sometimes months or even years) following death are similar to those around birth—schedules do not make sense and all life becomes a kind of vortex. If you have been the primary caregiver, you may find that you are no longer the point person, and this is a good time for someone else to take over. Alternately, you may be the one continuing to lead the way. No matter what, your hands will feel empty after all that concentrated physical care. Knitting, digging in the soil, or just having a small stone or piece of soft cloth in your pocket to rub might help occupy your hands and help ease some of the physical loss.

You never know quite how you are going to feel after a death. In regard to the body, you may want to be done with it as soon as possible—or you may feel a kind of attachment to it. Throughout history, humans have either tried to preserve the body (mummification or embalming), or wanted to thoroughly remove the body by means of a swift burial or fire. In any case, I encourage you (the caregiver) and those who are closest to the deceased person to do some slow and spacious work with the body.

HOME FUNERALS AND BODY CARE

Home funerals can feel very natural, even easy, if there is some degree of advance planning and if the loved one has died at home. If the death is unexpected or has occurred outside of the home or residence, a few more logistics will need to take place, such as transportation. Home funerals are legal in every state in the United States and Canada, although in a handful of states and provinces a funeral director must be hired to oversee.

Though home funerals are no longer considered routine, they are gaining popularity. Like so many trending topics of death-care, home funerals and home or green burials that are portrayed in magazines and on social media are in spacious, bright, privileged, sometimes affluent places. I wish to encourage the intimacy of a family-directed funeral to be as convenient as it can possibly be. A home funeral can be held in a messy apartment, at a neighbor's house, or in a very small backyard; it does not need to look a particular way. Wildflowers can be just as lovely as those from a floral shop, perhaps even more charming—and certainly more intimate. Some people may prefer—or rejoice in—having a licensed funeral director and a funeral home to rely upon. That's okay too—after-death and funeral care should never look one way. Culture, family customs, individuality, and context should be the considerations rather than societal expectations. Education and story sharing lead to empowered decision-making, and this is easier done in advance of a death.

If the deceased will remain in the home for a gathering, wash and dress the body, clean the room, and get a good flushing of fresh air into the space. Lay out the body on clean sheets for viewing or gather some lovely, soft boughs such as cedar to place the body on. If the body will go to a funeral home, you can do all this in a ceremony before the undertakers arrive. Even if you just comb your loved one's hair or wash their face and hands, it will feel like you have done *something* after so much attentive care through the dying process.

As you handle the body, you will begin to understand kinesthetically that the life energy is gone. However, it's still appropriate to talk to the body of your loved one: "I'm going to move your arm now," or, "I picked out your favorite shirt." As you bathe and dress the body, it can be awkward in a number of ways. You may feel extraordinarily clumsy, you may laugh, you may fall onto the body and cry. If the body is stiffening, you might need to cut the back of the clothing so that it fits onto the body more easily. All of this is okay. Depending on the size of the body, you may need two or more people to comfortably dress your loved one (using the rolling technique you used to move the person from side to side in bed when they were alive).

You may have an opportunity to help dig the grave, push the button at the crematory, or escort the body to the final place of disposition. Research or ask a modern death doula about the various ways of participating in the disposition. In the United States and Canada, there are greener types of disposition available in certain states and provinces that might appeal to you or your family. Again, sometimes these considerations are easier to research, contemplate, and arrange before the actual death.

If the body is sent off to refrigeration for the night or must travel without the direct care of loved ones, you may wish to tuck a piece of rose quartz in the deceased's pocket, attach a small bundle of protective herbs to their clothing, or lay a special blanket over the body. The idea is less that you are protecting the body *from* something or someone and more that you are attaching a bit of your love—a bit of remembrance—to the body that served your loved one on this planet.

Several families I have worked with have built caskets, hand carved the lowering or transport board for a green burial, or hand sewed their loved one's shroud. One family put in the work of building a coffin for their father out of old doors. What a creative use of the random things kept around old country farmhouses. Putting in work doesn't mean you need to create some kind of elaborate ceremony or disposition. Even the simplest acts of care for the body can feel like a kind of closing ceremony. If you do absolutely nothing? Well, that's fine too.

With slower deaths that allow you to digest a bit as you go along, many caregivers come out on the other side feeling like the experience was life-changing in a positive way. Of course, some say they *never* want to go through that experience again. But those who do want to do it again might begin to think of themselves as a grassroots or ancient death doula. Some may go on to do the certificate training to become a modern death doula and work in a professional setting or guide and encourage others to care for their own dying and dead.

Through anger, confusion, frustration, sorrow, resentment, exhaustion, elation, joy, and stillness, the completion of a life cycle is the end of a long ceremony.

📍 Alternative Location

Let's say that after all the home-death planning, your loved one ends up dying in a hospital. You can still take some time to sit with the body, use a washcloth to clean their face and hands, and (in some cases) fully wash and dress your loved one. Don't be shy about expressing your wishes—and be sure to ask the person with the greatest authority.

These small acts can be done whether or not a funeral home will pick up the body. This is still *your* loved one, your responsibility (even in death), and if you are next of kin, you have rights that accompany this.

SHOULD THE DEAD ATTEND THEIR OWN FUNERALS?

As an ancient and modern death doula, funeral celebrant, and family directed funeral guide in Vermont, I regularly aid in bridging the dead to their living by supporting home and green burials. These intimate hours that I spend with families teaching them how to roll, bathe, dress, shroud, transport, and bury their loved ones is some of the most cherished work that I do. Because family-directed funerals are not the norm, there is a lot of behind-the-scenes correspondence that I do talking with doctors, hospice staff, and town clerks. Knowing all of the work that went into connecting the legal dots to make it happen makes the actual ceremony feel more like it was the stars in the heavens that were connected.

Being with the body is not for everyone but, for some, it can help normalize something that doesn't feel good. Death does not feel good. However, the longer you spend in a room with a body, the longer your mind starts to wander a bit. And you begin, slowly, to possibly engage with something other than complete despair. Someone might share a funny memory, and for a split second you smile. Every funeral is different, but some I have attended or officiated have been quite joyous— and they are always better with the deceased present. At times, the body is *unable* to be present at the funeral or gathering (instances of missing people or plane crashes); these are tremendously sad affairs and often leave loved ones with a lack of closure.

We also must not forget that the act of having a funeral at all can be quite sacred and even a privilege. Not everyone gets a funeral—for a variety of reasons, including lack of funds, the inconvenience, or simply because there are no family members or friends to provide one. I also hear too often from those in older generations, "No, I don't want a funeral." This saddens me sometimes, as funerals are more for the *living* to gather, to mourn, to love one another, and to feel alive. Millennials and those younger seem to be the complete opposite and are looking forward to elaborate funerals!

Not so far back in our U.S. history, African American funerals of the enslaved were a central part of their lives. This was sometimes the only way they were able to gather, with some degree of autonomy, in "hush harbors" outside the enslaver's control. Unfortunately, quite often they were forbidden from gathering for a funeral, and many of the enslaved were denied a proper burial. Read more on this in Suzanne Smith's book *To Serve the Living: Funeral Directors and the African American Way of Death.*

How we mourn with a body matters greatly.

THE GOOD FUNERAL

Iain MacHarg, a bagpiper in Vermont, shared his sentiments with me:

As a Highland piper, I play a lot of funerals, memorial services, and end-of-life events. One trend that has been very noticeable is the absence of the decedent. Many families seem to be opting for cremation (therefore, no coffin); but more often than not, there isn't even an urn present. Many of the memorial services are really just people speaking about the deceased person. This seems to me a far cry from the funerals I attended as a youth, and certainly very far indeed from the "old world" wakes I attended. In the modern world, we seem to have a great fear of death and we don't want to see it or be reminded of it. As a result, the dead don't often attend the funeral.

I also interviewed a very kind funeral director about his work. His sentiments really struck me as true:

Having now been a funeral director for the past thirty-eight years in central Vermont, I have witnessed first-hand a migration of change in rituals. In the early days of my vocation, we began by taking the deceased back home for a day(s) visitation and viewing, family and friends crying, laughing, remembering, and saying goodbye. The following day, we went in procession from the home to the church, then to the graveyard, accompanying the dead through their service and burial, then to the reception. Today, a majority of families want services to be convenient, simple, inexpensive, and overwhelmingly absent of the dead—a celebration of life where we can be reflectively happy, avoiding pain and sorrow at all cost. We have created an idea of filling these events with activities and slideshows, balloon- and dove-releases, anecdotal storytelling of happy times, but there is one thing missing: the dead. Somehow we have come to the conclusion as a community that even though funerals are about the dead and for the living, the dead are uninvited to the gathering. The corpse, in whatever form, has become the proverbial "Debbie Downer." Let's avoid the sorrow, let's be happy and celebrate, let's put the fun in funeral. It's as if once the death takes place, the dead are whisked away and become ancillary to the event.

I would propose that we consider looking deeper into returning to the time-honored traditions of honoring our dead. I would advocate that a "good funeral" is comprised of four components: the deceased (in whatever form they wish), the mourners (our family and friends), the remembrance (a gathering where we honor and remember the dead), and the disposition (accompanying the dead to the ground or fire). These components can be achieved as elaborately or simply as one may wish. It can be as basic as accompanying the dead to the cemetery or crematory where we stand, reflect, and then bear witness to the cremation or burial (hence the good funeral: body, mourners, remembrance, disposition).

HERBS FOR REMEMBRANCE AND CEREMONY

There are many cultural traditions and rituals that use flowers, herbs, and plants to create ceremony or mark the death of an individual. Herbs, at this stage, do not need to be ingested. Instead, many can be burned as incense, placed on or around the body, steeped in warm water as a wash for the skin, or put in the casket at the time of cremation or burial. Oils can be used for anointing the forehead, feet, or entire body of the deceased and for blessing their journey.

What are the ancestral traditions of the one who is transitioning out of life? Connecting with one's cultural origins can be a satisfying way to acknowledge ancestors and bring a sense of peace—particularly if there was a traumatic break in these traditions due to colonialism, slavery, war, or estrangement from one's family.

Death makes us contemplate our past and question what will be in our future. If you allow this time of wonder, introspection, and longing to connect with both your past and future self, this can be a tremendously healing time. Plants, herbs, resins, and ceremony are ways to connect you to your ancestral roots. It's never too late to make an offering in this way.

The following is just a brief glimpse into the rich world of postmortem herbal care and rituals. Let this open your mind to explore more.

- **Lavender** essential oil and the **Thieves** blend both smell wonderful, are antibacterial, and can be used to bathe and oil the body after death.
- **Marigolds** are often found in abundance at rites of passage in India.
- **Garlic** braids and bunches of **yarrow** are used for protection in Celtic pagan tradition as one travels to the other side.
- **Rosemary** is an herb long used for remembrance in the Mediterranean.

- **Evergreens** symbolize everlasting energy/growth, hope, renewal, and life through winter's cold, dark cloak. (This is especially useful when other plants are under snow and ice.)
- **Chrysanthemums** are symbolic of death and used only as funeral flowers in much of France, Italy, Spain, Croatia, Hungary, and Poland.
- **Rose** is a nostalgic scent that is often pleasing. Roses can be planted in memory of the deceased, and bouquets can be given to those who are mourning so that they can dry and save them.
- **Lemon balm** can be uplifting. Serve it as a tea to those who are visiting the dying or to mourners at a funeral.
- **Peach** leaf tea is a traditional remedy for extreme agitation. In parts of the American South it is served to someone who is about to receive difficult news.
- **Linden** leaves and flowers are known as a calming heart tonic and can be perfect during times of grief.
- **Cinnamon** was used by Egyptians for anointing and embalming before mummification, in order to attain immortality.
- **Birch** is associated with reincarnation and rebirth. Write well-wishes or notes to your loved one on a birch bark scroll and place it in the casket, burn it in a ceremony, or send it with the body for cremation.
- **Trees** are planted on or near gravesites by the Bakongo people of the Republic of Congo; the growing roots symbolize the journey of a soul to the other world.
- **Lotus** flowers symbolize purity or reincarnation, rebirth and renewal.

- **Tulsi,** also known as holy basil, is native to India. By increasing vitality and well-being, it can be helpful for those grieving.
- **White roses**—as well as **lilies, irises,** and **chrysanthemums** in white or yellow—are considered funeral flowers in Chinese culture.
- **Cedar** is used for purification, to ward off negativity, and to stimulate a weary mind.
- **Palo santo** is a holy wood used by indigenous people of the Amazon. When burned, it can help with meditation, protection, and connecting with the divine. *Note that palo santo is currently endangered and should be used only in limited quantities—matchstick sized pieces—and exclusively for sacred work.*
- **Sandalwood** is an ancient tree from which incense and oil can be made. It increases energetic vibration, purification, and relaxation. *Use only in very small quantities unless ethically cultivated, as most varieties are endangered or vulnerable.*
- **Frankincense**—when made into incense or oil—can be used to increase spiritual awareness and boost intuition. *Note that these trees are threatened at this time.*

You can always make up your own combination of special herbs, flowers, and rituals for your specific ceremony. All traditions came from someone somewhere who wanted to create a special ceremonial remembrance. You have this power as well.

MOVING WITH GRIEF

You may work with your grief for quite some time, maybe for the rest of your life. Rather than seeing it as something to "get through" and "move on" from, learn how these new feelings incorporate into your life. Death changes life—that's what it does. Be gentle with yourself and others as you learn this new being you are becoming.

Under the pressure of sadness, you may find you have hardly any inspiration or imagination or even the slightest inkling what to *do* or how to *be*. You might barely be able to match your socks, let alone think of a creative way to soothe yourself. Men, in particular, can be challenged in feeling, revealing, and working with their grief; they tend to be looked to as pillars of support for others. Regardless of your gender, if you do not have good role models—family and friends who have worked with their grief in productive and inspiring ways—you can look for ideas in other times and cultures. We can learn from other traditions, incorporating practices that fit with our lifestyle and beliefs—without culturally appropriating their customs.

I find many Jewish traditions surrounding death to be poignant. Some Jewish people sit shiva in the home of the deceased for seven days (though today some are shortening that). During this time, those who are mourning do not work or attend gatherings, and they forfeit other kinds of entertainment and vanities. A candle is lit, prayers recited, and the general idea is to sit in grief and in closeness with others. A way of adapting this into something you can practice is simply to make a conscious decision to remove yourself from the routine of life and allow yourself to mourn at home. Make a ritual out of lighting a candle and keeping it lit for the time that you are mourning at home, and recite the kinds of prayers or poetry that mean something to you or the one who has died.

Here are some suggestions for moving with grief:

- **Try vocalizing your grief.** Keening has been a tradition in Ireland and Gaelic Scotland for centuries. This death wail, or lamenting, has been practiced around the globe throughout history, including by cultures in Asia, West Africa, the Americas, and Australia. In Ireland, professional mourners were hired to wail loudly or sing their sorrow at the funeral or wake, oftentimes on their knees, rocking back and forth. This triggered—or allowed—others to vocalize their sadness. To me, we do not do enough wailing in our society; we hardly allow our toddlers to do it. At a Death & Dying Symposium I coordinated, I experimented by hiring a bagpiper to play for us while we practiced our own keening exercises. To my surprise and slight disappointment, no one really let loose. Though we all cried collectively about our individual losses, it didn't amount to wailing. Perhaps there is a difference when a group is mourning the same loss. Or perhaps we have the potential to be stifled in our grief, and this is why professionals have been hired in the past to start the process. To me, a good loud wind movement from your lungs can be as helpful as a good earth movement from your bowels.

- **Tell the story of your loved one's death.** Every death has a story; telling it over and over again will align the ineffable experience you felt in your bones and your being and help form it into words to make it feel real and more natural. There is a play between body, mind, and being (or spirit) when processing feelings of loss. The stories of death need to be spoken into the earthly plane, from mouth to ear to heart. As you speak to people about your experience, you may find yourself saying things or recalling bits that you previously did not remember. When sharing, someone may ask you, "When your mother was dying did she talk about seeing anyone who had previously died?" You may suddenly remember, "Oh yes! She said her father was there!" If you cannot find a listening ear, or if you sense mistrust or are experiencing embarrassment about your feelings, try talking to a clergy person, a bereavement group, a kind stranger, an animal, or a tree. Trees are very good listeners.

- **Sleep.** Rest may help more than anything, at least for the first little while.
- **Dance, walk or run.** Moving the body moves stagnant energy.
- **Play music, make music.** Old favorites can be comforting, but also try new kinds of music to see what fits now as you grieve.
- **Go to the water, sit in water, move in water.** Add copious amounts of Epsom salts to your bath to draw out all the stiffness and toxins that need to escape from your body. If you do not have a tub, stand in a large pot of water in the shower and pour Epsom salts into the pot along with a few drops of essential oil.
- **Lie down on the earth, put your hands in the earth, and water the earth with your tears.**

- **Stargaze.** On a clear night, lie on your back and look at the stars. (If you are in a city you might have to get creative). Play games with the stars. Count them. Can you see all of them? If you hold your gaze in one place, can you see stars in the periphery that seem to disappear when you turn to look at them? Can you find the constellations? Using a telescope can be a phenomenal experience, but lying on your back can be therapeutically grounding.

- **Open your mind to a whole new world.** Just as with the "big view, little view" suggestions for children in the previous chapter, using a magnifying glass can open you up to a whole new world. You can easily keep a magnifying glass in your pocket. Examine the backs of leaves and follow the tiny veins or look at a bug up close. If you have a microscope, start collecting random items from your environment to inspect.

- **Go to the animals.** They ask you no questions and do not need a particular response from you. If you do not have your own pets, ask to spend time with a friend's pet. Visit a rescue or therapy farm, take a horseback riding lesson, or just go somewhere to watch wild animals in their own habitat.

- **Make an everyday routine into a ritual.** Mindfulness and attention to detail may become a relief. Even preparing a cup of tea can be made into a ritual when your every movement is precise and focused in the moment. For a nice invigorating and healing tea, mix fresh grated ginger, turmeric, lemon, and honey into your hot water. Add a touch of cayenne if you like spice. Find your perfect mixture.

- **Try physically balancing your body.** Since childhood, I have walked on a tightwire—and I use balance as a form of meditation. Keeping my concentration on minute movements helps free me from agitation or heavy matters of the mind or heart. The same can be done on the floor just by shifting your weight back and forth from foot to foot, feeling deeply the small and slow physical movements. Tai chi or yoga can also be good for this.

- **Create an absent-minded sensation.** Sand drawings and beach play can be therapeutic. Add shells, sticks, rocks, or flowers; then let it wash away. It can feel good to build things up, to use care and attention, and then let it go. This is different from the feeling you get when someone nonchalantly destroys your careful work. (Although that can be a good practice in impermanence, I don't think it has the same therapeutic benefits.)

- **Swing.** If moving and rocking feel good to you, go to a playground and sit on a swing. If you can find an adult-size swing set, even better. On the back-swing breathe in, on the forward-swing breathe out. Then try the reverse: breathe out on the back-swing and breathe in on the forward-swing (all while pumping your legs). If you find yourself getting lightheaded, slow it way down, inhaling during a complete back-and-forth swing and exhaling on the next one. You can do this same exercise just sitting on your couch at home and rocking very slowly.

- **Paint a new image of your loved one's death.** Art—your own or others—might help. Some deaths are less than ideal for many reasons. Even if you're reading this book in order to care for a loved one who is slowly dying at home, they may end up dying suddenly from a fall instead. If the last time you saw your loved one was traumatic for you, ask an artist to help paint a new image of their death. An artist might be able to help soften a disturbing image. You can keep this painting or image private, if you wish, and take it out to view and breathe with when you need it.

⚜ **Take time with your loved one's belongings.** It's okay to smell your loved one's items and hold them close: cry into their blankets and smell their soap, deodorant, or perfume. It can be very difficult to pack up or give away belongings. Additionally, you might learn things about your loved one that you previously did not know, and this can be painful— or sometimes humorous. Go slow. Bring home a box of the bare essentials to engage with privately. Look for ways to transform some of their belongings in order to incorporate them into your own life. Jewelry or pillowcases can be made from a loved one's clothing; cremains can be made into glass pendants, window ornaments, or paperweights.

⚜ **Walk a labyrinth.** Walking labyrinths can be a helpful way to discover answers to asked questions, contemplate your current situation, and think about life and death. Labyrinths can be found at churches across the world, in ancient sacred spaces, and in children's play areas. They are not to be confused with mazes, where you can get lost: a labyrinth has no dead ends, and when you come to the middle (the halfway point) you simply walk back out the way you came.

I interviewed my former father-in-law, Sig Lonegren, a dowser, geomancer, and author of *Labyrinths: Ancient Myths and Modern Uses,* about the use of labyrinths when working with death and grief. He replied, "Walking the labyrinth can be done to address almost any problem, including issues around life and death. When one is in touch with the Spiritual Realms, the labyrinth can provide much comfort. Walking labyrinths can provide clarity and comfort in both directions—your past, and what is to come as you approach the end of this life. It is an excellent walking meditation tool."

- **Choose a new route.** While habit is good sometimes, it can also be beneficial to switch things up. If you always walk a certain route, reverse the direction. If you always eat at a certain restaurant, try a new one.

- **Throw a good punch.** The first time I was taught how to properly punch and kick a punching bag, I was elated. Not all deaths leave us feeling sad. Sometimes we are extremely angry, and moving some of that anger physically can provide relief. (See the mindfulness practice below about throwing punches and shooting arrows—both of which can be therapeutic.)

- **Have a second funeral.** I encourage having a funeral at the time of the death—even if it is an uncoordinated jumble. I also think second funerals are helpful for healing.

- **Cry.** If tears won't come, try to stimulate them without thinking directly about your deceased or dying loved one. Watch a sad movie, read a sad book, listen to sad music, even chop some onions to stimulate the tear ducts and get things flowing. Tears might not come immediately, or they might come at the strangest time. Don't stop them—even if it happens at an inconvenient moment. Let them flow, even if you are in the middle of a business meeting or in a grocery store. Tell the people around you, "I need to cry." If you are driving, pull over to a safe place and have a good cry. The car is actually a great place to scream, cry, and bawl. It's a small, relatively soundproof mobile nest and can feel safe.

⚜

MINDFULNESS PRACTICE

Throwing Punches and Shooting Arrows

Before beginning this practice, learn how to punch properly so that you don't injure yourself! Start with soft punches until you learn the resistance of the object you are striking—whether it's a pillow or a punching bag.

Take a deep breath. Notice the anger in your body. Where do you feel it? Where is it originating from in your body?

With feet flat on the ground, draw energy from the earth, pull it up through your body, through the place of anger and resistance, and let it run out your arm to your fist as you strike. Imagine that your anger blasted through your knuckles and into the punching bag.

Repeat as many times as you'd like (remembering that even a proper punch can leave your hand bruised and your muscles aching).

A similar exercise can be done shooting an arrow.

Notice the anger, aggression, or sadness in your body. With an inhale, draw up energy from the earth. Let it meet and move straight through the anger in your body.

While drawing back the bow, let the energy flow into the arrow, and with a sharp out-breath release the arrow.

I trained in a twelfth-century Japanese mindfulness practice called *kyudo* and found it therapeutic when using it as a form of moving energy. In the kyudo practice, you thank the target after it receives the arrow.

. . . .

Special note: If your grief and sadness become a long-lasting depression and/or you have feelings of ending your own life, please seek help from *humans* (instead of trying solely to help yourself or seeking internet help). We are not meant to grieve alone—though oftentimes our society does not make that apparent. A welcoming place to start is to find a bereavement support group, which hospice or your local hospital can guide you to. Or, if you are feeling scared that you may end your life, please call 911 or the Suicide and Crisis Lifeline: 988.

. . . .

Meditation for Dissolving
into the Elements

*T*he Buddhist dissolution practice is beautiful; it inspired my version of it here. My husband, Pablo, a transpersonal therapist and accomplished meditation instructor, contributed the section about space, which is a wonderful addition.

You can do this meditation by yourself to help you relate to the dying process. It can also be done with the one who is dying, if an awareness practice might be helpful and your loved one seems interested.

Situate yourself in a comfortable position. This could mean lying down or sitting. (It is not to be done standing.) The intention for this meditation is total relaxation. If you are in a hurry or anxious, take a few moments to return to your breath (see page 65). Also, if this meditation ever begins to cause you anxiety, simply stop the exercise. Take some deep breaths and perhaps have a drink of water.

Read the following aloud, leaving space and time between

each element and maintaining a slow cadence throughout. Pauses are indicated where you may wish to take some slow breaths. You can practice this dissolution of elements meditation just once or a couple of times in a row. Once you are familiar with this exercise, close your eyes and continue silently; you can make up your own words and imagery as you go.

Earth

You are an earth body. Your body is thick, heavy, rich, and fertile. Feel the shape of your body firm as earth, made of soil and in the soil. [Pause.] Feel each particle of soil in the earth-body formation, and then slowly allow the shape of your body to lose form. Slowly the shape of your face, the curve of each foot, relaxes beautifully, whole in its disintegration, nutrient-rich in its merging with the rest of the earth. [Pause.] No longer a body.

Water

You are a water body. Your body is flowing, moving, drifting, moist. Feel the shape of your body as water, in an ocean of water. [Pause.] Feel each molecule of oxygen and hydrogen in the water-body formation moving with the ebb and flow and pull of the moon. Slowly allow the shape of your body to comfortably lose form and merge with all other ocean water. [Pause.] No longer a body.

Fire

You are a fire body. Your body is hot, pulsating, charged, fed by the fuel of earthly attachment. Feel the shape of your body as fire, crackling and combusting in open space. [Pause.] Feel each element that creates the heat and changes the shape of your fire body. Slowly the core of your body and your limbs separate, become sparks, flicks of light, and peacefully merge into the cosmic element of fire. [Pause.] No longer a body.

Air

You are an air body. Your body is swirling, rushing, inhaling, exhaling. Feel the shape of your body as air surrounded by air. [Pause.] Feel each particle of pure oxygen that creates your air body, then allow the shape of your body to gently lose form. Slowly the shape of your being separates from itself and merges with all oxygen everywhere. [Pause.] No longer a body.

Space

You are space beyond body, space that is vast, luminous, fearless, and free. Feel the formless space that exists externally beyond the elements of your body. [Pause.] Feel the limitless expanse in all directions as your elements merge with the universal essence that knows no time, shape, form, or sense of self. [Pause.] No longer a body.

The Ancient and Modern Death Doula

I never would have expected that death would be the thing to bring me back to life.

ALUA ARTHUR

WHAT IS A DEATH DOULA?

The work of a death doula is a way of life—how we care for others, how we care for ourselves, the uncomfortable conversations we allow ourselves to engage in, how we confront our own mortality, and how we choose to live our lives.

Death doulas want to create (or maintain) the kind of environment that feels comfortable to die in. This environment could pertain to just the person dying but can include their family and friends as well. Think that's a tall order? It can be! This means getting paperwork in order, creating a schedule that feels manageable, engaging in difficult conversations, nonjudgmentally witnessing emotional unraveling, attending appointments, house cleaning, creating flow in the care area, assisting with ethical wills, sitting vigil, offering spiritual support, providing physical care, and lots of listening. Not every death doula does all of these things, but some do all of that and more.

ANCIENT ROOTS
AND MODERN PRACTICES

Though the word *doula*—meaning "female servant" or "female slave"—originated in ancient Greece, there have been individuals who assist the entering and exiting of life for as long as there have been humans on earth. This kind of care is ancient and not specific to any one culture or place on earth; it belongs to everyone and no one.

Presently, I see a divide in the death doula world—to the point where I think there need to be two different names for these paths. There are those of us who desire a societal shift in our approach to death and dying and are really working to reclaim deathcare whether or not we have had formal training, and there are those who seek a new profession that requires a certificate in death doula training. I see a need for both of these paths; I refer to them as the *ancient death doula* and the *modern death doula*.

The death doulas in centuries past used their hands, their hearts, and whatever resources they had access to, to assist their loved ones through death. They learned by *doing,* since this way of life was modeled in their own homes and communities. There are people today who are *remembering* and wish to reclaim this half of life that has been forgotten by so many. Without death, they understand that life is only half lived. These are the ancient death doulas who have heard the call of their ancestors, and they are arriving spiritually aware, empathic, with mortar and pestle in hand and herbs tucked in their aprons.

What is new in recent decades are families stretched out across the planet, mazes of paperwork from lawyers and banks, healthcare hurdles, the pressures of productivity, and 24/7 connectivity to *everything* from the phones in our pockets.

Modern death doulas can assist with some of these things because they are trained to know the system. Though they are not lawyers or therapists or medical professionals, their certificate training should have taught them how to help navigate those challenges and to point the one dying (or the client doing advance work) in the right direction. They may also be able to help create a manageable schedule and offer reminders about self-care and disconnecting from the demands of the outside world.

Should you choose to pursue formal death doula training, the program should emphasize a doula's role within the broader community of care (which includes hospice workers, chaplains, and social workers among others). There are communities where people have been doing this work for a long time, though not under the title of "death doula." In the American South, for example, there are many women of color who have been doing death doula work for generations, trained within their own families (perhaps in addition to nursing or nursing assistant training). They do not require an external resource to validate their deathcare.

The point of death doula training is not to reinforce your existing feelings and beliefs; nor is it to validate who you are as a human being. To feel, recognize, and move through your own stuck places, judgments, and fears; to release into the spaciousness of an open sky that can hold the weather systems of others—that is where the essence of a death doula's service resides. Whether or not you choose to care for others while they are dying, the right death doula training can feel very healing and inspiring and can ignite a fresh appreciation for your own life. Death doula trainings are all very different. Research carefully to find the one that feels like the best fit for you. A few suggestions to consider are provided in the resources list following this chapter.

I teach community deathcare to my students, many of whom are already professionals in their fields. Doctors and nurses whose education was devoid of care for the dying, therapists who wish to better speak with their clients who have life-threatening or terminal diagnoses, aestheticians, barbers, baristas, all of whom are excellent in how they serve the world come to the Village Deathcare training. They recognize that learning about deathcare will enhance not just their work and livelihood but their own lives as they become more appreciative of living fully.

DREAMS OF A SOCIETY THAT EMBRACES DEATHCARE

If deathcare has never been modeled in a way for you to see, then death doula training is a great way to learn about healthy holistic care for the dying. Certificate training can be a really good thing, as we are desperate for healthcare workers nation-wide. However, we cannot let the availability and popularity of certificate-based deathcare become the Band-Aid solution for caring for our dying.

Being a caregiver for the dying is not only a lost art but a lost value. The reminder of death is the strongest, most important reminder of life. However, with the slow deaths hidden from us (in nursing homes or acute care facilities) and regular exposure to violent deaths in movies, video games, and media showing mass shootings, we are not easily able to connect with death being natural or even kind. If we have never touched death gently, it's hard to experience death comfortably as part of life.

We need a societal shift toward valuing family-based and/or neighborhood and community care for the dying and the deceased. Even if one cannot care for their loved one at home, paid leave from work to attend to a loved one's deathcare should be a right. I believe these discussions should be debated as heavily as healthcare in governmental platforms. Deathcare *is* actually healthcare.

Resources for Death, Dying, and Stretching Your Mind

DEATH AND DYING

Death Doula Training and Teachers

Anne-Marie Keppel (author), Village Deathcare Citizen, villagedeathcare.com

Lashanna Williams, A Sacred Passing, asacredpassing.org

Sarah Kerr, Centre for Sacred Deathcare, sacreddeathcare.com

Podcasts and YouTube Channels

Joél Simone Maldonado, *The Grave Woman* YouTube channel

Karen Wyatt, M.D., *End-of-Life University* podcast

National Home Funeral Alliance, *A Path Home* podcast

Websites

Collective for Radical Death Studies, radicaldeathstudies.com

Green Burial Council, greenburialcouncil.org

National End of Life Doula Alliance, nedalliance.org

National Home Funeral Alliance, homefuneralalliance.org

Recommended Reading

Touching upon Your Own Mortality

Being with Dying by Joan Halifax

Societal Views

All works by Clarissa Pinkola Estés

Being Mortal by Atul Gawande

Die Wise by Stephen Jenkinson

God's Hotel by Victoria Sweet

Man's Search for Meaning by Viktor Frankl

Grief and Sorrow

My Father's Wake by Kevin Toolis

The Smell of Rain on Dust by Martín Prechtel

Wild Edge of Sorrow by Francis Weller

Spiritual Support

All works by Pema Chödrön

To Bless the Space Between Us by John O'Donohue

Preparing to Die by Andrew Holecek

7 Lessons for Living from the Dying by Karen Wyatt

Spirit Speaker by Salicrow

Tibetan Book of Living and Dying by Sogyal Rinpoche

Ancestry

Ancestral Medicine by Daniel Foor

End of Life Enchiridion by Anne-Marie Keppel

Growth Rings by Anne-Marie Keppel

Helpful Viewpoints

Confessions of a Funeral Director by Caleb Wilde

Cultivating the Doula Heart by Francesca Lynn Arnoldy

From Here to Eternity by Caitlin Doughty

Life, Death, Grief, and the Possibility of Pleasure by Oceana
  Sawyer

Making Friends with Death by Judith L. Lief

Smoke Gets in Your Eyes by Caitlin Doughty

This Party's Dead by Erica Buist

Ceremony, Home Funerals, and Natural Burial

The After-Death Care Educator Handbook by Lee Webster

Changing Landscapes compiled and edited by Lee Webster

Final Rights by Joshua Slocum and Lisa Carlson

Home Funeral Ceremonies by Donna Belk and
  Kateyanne Unullisi

A Lighter Approach

Good Mourning by Elisabeth Meyer

Spook by Mary Roach

Stiff by Mary Roach

On Race and Racism in End-of-Life Care

Till Death Do Us Part by Allan Amanik and Kami Fletcher

Medical Apartheid by Harriet A. Washington

To Serve the Living by Suzanne E. Smith

Books on Death for Children

In addition to the picks below, this website is a good resource:
https://whatsyourgrief.com/childrens-books-about-death

Grandpa's Stories by Joseph Coelho

The Invisible String by Patrice Karst

Lifetimes by Bryan Mellonie and Robert Ingpen

Tear Soup by Pat Schwiebert and Chuck DeKlyen

For Young Budding Death Doulas

Beneath the Bone Tree by Anne-Marie Keppel

The Death of Faefolk by Anne-Marie Keppel

The Rabbit Listened by Cori Doerrfeld

STRETCHING YOUR MIND

Online

Center for Humane Technology, humanetech.com

Daniel Schmachtenberger, various online interviews

Recommended Reading

I recommend all works by Andrew Holecek and Sophie Strand as well as books, talks, and retreats by Tsultrim Allione, in addition to the following titles.

Black and Buddhist by Pamela Ayo Yetunde and Cheryl Giles

A New Earth by Eckhart Tolle

The Way to Love by Anthony de Mello

Music

Hz frequencies for alleviating stress—many beautiful versions are available through YouTube, as are soothing ambient nature sounds such as ocean waves, a summer night, a crackling fire

Music and written works about Hildegard von Bingen; classical music, such as Bach, Brahms, Mozart, Boccherini; modern-day classical cellists Yo-Yo Ma and Adam Hurst

Psychic Mediums

Mary Beth Bruce, (617) 710-2228

Salicrow, salicrow.com

About the Author

Anne-Marie Keppel is an ancient and modern death doula, community death-care educator, certified Life-Cycle funeral celebrant, and Feeding Your Demons facilitator. She holds Master teacher-level training in Reiki, is a trained nurse assistant, lifelong meditator, and professional event coordinator. A mother of three, she lives in the Northeast Kingdom of Vermont. Learn more about Anne-Marie's work as a death doula and her community deathcare training programs at **StardustMeadow.com** or **AnneMarieKeppel.com**.

. . . .

Vignette of a Life's Story

My specialties as a human are in heart, intuition, mindfulness, practicalities, sensitivities, braveness in vulnerability, never-ending curiosity, and the belief that magic can happen at any moment—and often does. Everything that I teach is based on my own experiences.

I had an idyllic childhood spent in the hills of Vermont with my family's horses, cats, dogs, and other creatures and spent summers performing in a youth circus. I attended my first series of Celtic Shamanism workshops at the age of sixteen and was attuned to Reiki (thanks to my brilliant mother, a Reiki Master teacher) when I was seventeen. My education was enhanced by nightly fireside stories, teachings, and contemplations with my parents. They shared with me their work with children, studies in psychology, and neuro-linguistic programming (NLP) and EMDR therapy techniques—all of it served up with an overarching spiritual recognition. These trainings, therefore, became deeply integrated into how I think and how I observe and process my world.

After becoming a mother at the age of nineteen, marrying, having a second child, and then divorcing at twenty-six, life became significantly more challenging. With shared custody, the torment of not having my two young children with me seven days a week, twenty-four hours a day, shattered my heart. For ten years I was a single mother and often had to choose between paying my electric bill and paying my car insurance. I found refuge in a Buddhist retreat center where everyone leaned *into* pain, sadness, and discomfort instead of ignoring it or trying to "cheer up," as so much of society told me I needed to do. I knew that the acknowledgment of my sorrow was the only way to heal.

I had been an event coordinator for a decade, but coordinating a weekend retreat for the Thirteen Indigenous Grandmothers was the crossover event that brought me to where I am today. Serving these holy indigenous women awakened in me a desire to serve the elderly. Soon after that time, it was my love and care for an elderly homeless man named Frank that set my life's work into motion and ignited my interest in community deathcare.

I greatly enjoyed my work as a hospice volunteer and as a licensed nurse assistant and private duty nurse for the elderly. Working in a small residential care facility, I was the only one on duty during overnight shifts. I loved the residents, and being alert in the silence of the night awakened a confidence and bravery in me that needed healing. I tuned into the cycles of the moon and changes in air pressure, since both of these would affect my shift. Both the full moon and new moon played a role in the residents' activity level and sleep patterns—sometimes meaning that the residents would page me more often for assistance or conversation. Drops in barometric pressure could cause headaches, confusion, and increased arthritic pain—requiring extra attention or pain relief medication. This was how my love of alternative medicine and herbal support grew alongside caregiving.

Today I live with my husband—love of my life—Pablo and our adorable little girl; my older two children live within easy driving distance. I feel like I am actually living my seventh life in this one lifetime. I engage in my world with awakened gratitude because I know nothing is permanent, yet this is where I am *now*—and *living* is a precious gift.

My great thanks to teachers, friends, and inspirations,
in no particular order: Pablo Coddou,
Chögyam Trungpa Rinpoche, Stephen Jenkinson,
Joan Halifax, Tsultrim Allione, Clarissa Pinkola Estés,
Andrew Holecek, Viktor Frankl, Anthony de Mello,
Cornelius and Theresa Keppel, Daniel Schmachtenberger,
Sarah Kerr, Alua Arthur, Salicrow, Jennifer and Susan,
Carey, Karen, in-laws, and my Village
Deathcare Citizen students.

Index